Dads of the Animal Kingdom

Protecting the Future

Shiva Kumar

Contents

Part III

Exploring Nature's Caretakers: The Great Dads Adventure

Hey there, young adventurers! I am the Sky, a huge, story-filled place all about courage and love. Get ready for a super fun journey to meet the coolest animal dads out there. These dads are exceptional at looking after their little ones.

Picture us flying way up high, ready to see how amazing our world is. We are going to check out lush green forests, bright, and sunny fields, and the deep, mysterious ocean. Along the way, we will meet twenty-one animal dads who are real-life heroes to their babies.

First up, we have a penguin dad who stands strong in freezing winds just for his baby. Then there is a monkey dad who gives piggyback rides to his little one wherever he goes. And do not forget the eagle dad, keeping a close eye on his nest from up high. These stories will show us just how much these dads adore their babies.

This trip is going to be a blast, but it is also a chance to see the world through the eyes of these caring dads. We will discover all the ways they shower their babies with love.

If you can, share this adventure with your dad or a grown-up who looks out for you. It is a cool way to learn about being kind and brave together.

Are you ready? Grab onto my cloud tails! Let us kick off our adventure and cheer on the super dads of the animal kingdom!

Part I

Emus, Silverback Gorillas, Emperor Penguins, Ospreys, American Alligators, Arctic Wolves, and Red Foxes.

Chapter 1 – The Emu's Tale: Heroes of the Australian Bush

Exploring the World of Emus

Australia's Big Bird

S ay hello to the Emu, the biggest bird in Australia.

As you look around Australia's wide spaces, you will see these large, lovely birds. Emus were important to the first people of Australia (Indigenous Australians). They respect Emus for their strength and for how they help the land.

What Makes Emus Special

Emus are great at living in Australia's wild places. They have long legs that let them run fast through woods and over sand. Guess what? Emu dads take care of their eggs and babies all by themselves. They are super dads!

The Emu's Dance

When an Emu dad wants to find a mom and have babies, he does a special dance. He puffs himself up and makes a muffled sound to win her heart. This dance happens under the big sky and shows he is ready to be an amazing dad. This is how they welcome the new baby Emus.

Emus at Home

Bush Explorers

Emus love to explore. They walk through forests and deserts in Australia, looking for food. They eat plants, seeds, and bugs. You can find Emus near the ocean or in the big, wild Outback. They are happy to have adventures and feel at home in many places.

An Emu's Day

Every day, Emus look for food. They walk fast with their long legs and use their beaks to pick up delicious things. Emus often walk by themselves, but sometimes they meet other Emus. They might find friends or a good place to rest. Watching Emus can be fun. They have their own way of talking and like to stay together.

The Important Job of Emu Dads

Building a Nest

In Australia's wide lands, Emu dads have a big job: they take care of their unborn chicks. First, the mom Emu makes a soft nest on the ground and lays her green eggs. She hides them with leaves and sticks. Then, it is dad's turn. He sits on the nest to keep the eggs warm and safe, showing his love for his future babies.

Watching Over the Nest

The Emu dad stays close to the nest. After the mom leaves, he keeps the eggs cozy. He does not eat; he just guards the eggs from wind and rain. It is challenging work, but he does it to help his chicks hatch safely.

Baby Emus Hatch

When the sun wakes up the land, it is time for baby Emus to hatch. They peek out at the world and take their first shaky steps. Their dad is there to protect and teach them. With his care, they grow stronger and learn to walk correctly.

Growing Up Wild

As the chicks get bigger, they get curious. Dad Emu shows them how to live in the wild, like finding food and staying away from danger. He is a patient teacher. Thanks to him, the Emu family learns to stick together and be ready for life's adventures.

Staying Safe in the Wild

Looking Out for Danger

In the wild parts of Australia, Emus must be careful. There are animals like dingoes, eagles, and foxes that might try to catch them. But Emu dads are always on guard. They watch over their chicks to keep them away from these dangers. And it is not just animals that can be a problem. Sometimes, places where people live can bother Emus too.

Overcoming Challenges

Emus are strong birds, even when life gets hard. They can run fast, which helps them escape danger and find food. Emus are good at living anywhere, whether it is green fields by the sea or the hot, dry middle of Australia. If their home changes because of what people do, they learn to deal with it. They show us how great they are at being brave and tough.

Growing Up as an Emu

From Chicks to Emus

Each day, the baby Emus grow a little more. With their dad's guidance, they change from tiny chicks into big, sturdy birds. Their feathers get shiny as they get older.

Learning the Wild Ways

Baby Emus have much to learn about the wild, and their dad serves as their primary teacher. He shows them the best spots to find delicious food and teaches them how to escape danger. These lessons make them strong and ready for life in the vast bushland of Australia.

Setting Off on Their Own

The young Emus move further as they grow, armed with their dad's wisdom to keep them safe. Eventually, the time comes for them to go out into the world by themselves. Dad Emu watches them go with pride and a touch of sadness, knowing they will carry his teachings with them.

Amazing Emu Dads

Emu Dads Are the Best

Emu dads are special. Instead of just leaving the egg sitting there, they act. They do everything to help their babies grow strong.

Emus in Old Australian Stories

People in Australia have always known Emu dads are amazing. The Indigenous Australians, who were the first people there, have stories about them. These stories say Emu dads are strong and good at taking care of their families and the land.

Why Do We Love Emu Dads?

- They sit with their eggs for a long time without eating, so they get thin.

- They keep their chicks safe from any danger.

- They find the best food and water for their chicks.

- Being a fantastic dad is essential for Emus. It helps them and their families live well in the wild.

- Emu dads are like the heroes of the Australian bush, showing everyone how to be strong and kind.

Fun with Emus

Be Creative:

Art: Draw or make an Emu. Show everyone how beautiful they are and where they live.

Stories: Write stories or poems about Emus. Then, tell everyone how impressive Emus are.

Keep Emus Safe:

Help: Join groups that protect Emus. You can plant trees or learn about Emus. This keeps them safe.

Learn and Share:

Discover Emus: Learn what Emus do and where they live. Share what you learn with your family and friends.

Save the Planet: Remember to recycle and not waste water. It helps the Earth and the Emus.

Science Help: Join projects that study Emus. You can make a significant difference to them.

When we do these things, we are not just having a fun time; we are also helping Emus and the Earth. It is great to learn, create, and help Emus stay happy in their homes.

Goodbye to the Emus

Emus: Amazing Birds of Australia

We have come to the end of our Emu adventure. We know now that Emus are more than just big birds in the Outback. They keep the land well and show us how powerful life can be. They remind us of Australia's long story.

Helping Emus

We should all care about these impressive birds. By helping Emus, we help other living things in Australia. Safe homes for Emus mean a happier place for everyone.

Remembering Emus

Let us not forget what Emus taught us about nature. Taking care of the land means we are taking care of Emus as well. This helps Emus stay with us for many more years and keeps Australia's wild heart beating.

Celebrating Emus

Let us give a cheer to Emus and always try to keep them and their homes safe!

Glossary

- **Bushland:** wild, natural areas covered with plants and trees.

- **Ecosystem:** A community of living things and their home, working together.

- **Emu:** A large, tall bird from Australia that cannot fly but can run fast.

- **Habitat:** The natural home of an animal or plant.

- **Indigenous Australians** were the first people to live in Australia. They are also known as Aboriginal Australians.

- **Nest:** a comfortable place where birds lay their eggs and take care of them.

- **Outback:** the vast, remote, and dry areas of Australia, far from cities.

- **Recycle:** to process used materials into new products to prevent waste.

- **Wilderness:** a natural area of land that is unaltered or ungoverned by humans

Chapter 2: Jungle Giants: Silverbacks in the Wild

Meet the Silverback Gorillas

Jungle Kings with Gentle Hearts

It is the huge silverback gorillas who rule the lush, green jungles of Africa.

Everyone looks up to them. Because they're more than just beautiful to look at. Also, it's because of how well they take care of their families. They are strong, but they use it carefully. This shows that they are watching over their family and home in the forest.

Why Silverbacks Are Amazing

Silverbacks are big and strong. They have fur that looks like silver. They talk and move in a certain way that makes them sound and look good to each other. Silverbacks are amazing because they show great leadership and care within their gorilla families.

Helping the Forest

Silverbacks help their home, the forest, by eating plants and fruits. This makes more plants grow. They teach us why we should take care of nature and its animals.

Living in the Jungle

Forest Homes

Silverbacks live where it is green and wild in Central Africa. They find food and cozy places to sleep in the jungle. They are experts at finding food and traveling through the trees.

A Day with Silverbacks

Silverbacks start the day looking for breakfast and water. Later, they rest and clean each other. At night, they sleep in nests, with the big silverback keeping them safe.

Gorilla Families

Gorillas live in family groups called troops. The big silverback is the leader who keeps them all safe. They care for each other, with the silverback looking after the moms and babies. They have their own way of talking with noises and body language.

The Silverback's Job

Leader and Keeper

The silverback is the head of the troop. He is the biggest and most looked up to. He makes sure everyone is safe and happy.

Guide and Decision-Maker

He helps find the best places for food and rest. He knows the jungle well and leads his family to good eating spots.

Teacher and Helper

He shows the younger gorillas how to stay safe. His teaching helps them learn to live on their own and makes the family strong.

Safe in the Jungle

Jungle Adventures

Jungles have dangers. But, the big, strong silverback gorilla makes sure his family is safe. He pays special attention to the baby gorillas.

Eyes Wide Open

The silverback gorilla keeps a close watch all the time. If he sees something bad, he tells his family. He is very brave and fights off any danger to keep them safe.

Protector of the Family

Silverbacks are super strong. They can run fast, yell, or show off their muscles to make scary animals go away. Their most important job is to keep their family safe.

A Gorilla's Love

Heart of the Family

Silverbacks are not leaders; they are very loving. They make sure their family feels safe, loved, and cozy.

Fun and Learning

Silverbacks are also very gentle when they play with the baby gorillas. They teach them new things through play, helping them to be happy as they grow.

Keeping Peace

Silverbacks help everyone get along. They stop fights and teach the gorillas to be nice to each other, keeping the family happy and strong.

Overcoming Trouble

Challenges Ahead

Sometimes, silverback gorillas and their families face big challenges. They may lose their home or be in danger from hunters. But the silverbacks always take care of their families no matter what.

Saving Their Home

It is important for us to help protect the homes of silverbacks. We should not cut down trees and should take care of our planet's climate and the land where they live.

How You Can Help Gorillas

Talk About Gorillas: Tell your friends and family cool things about gorillas. Use the internet to learn and share. This helps gorillas because more people will want to keep them safe.

Keep Learning: Read books or watch shows about gorillas. Share the fun facts you learn with others, like at school.

Be a Gorilla Hero: Choose to do things that are good for animals and the planet. We can all help make a better place for gorillas and other animals.

Have Fun with Gorillas

Watch Gorillas: Go to zoos or parks to see gorillas. Watch how they play and live together.

Virtual Safari: Use the internet to see where gorillas live. It is fun, like going on an adventure without leaving home.

Make Gorilla Art: Draw or craft something about gorillas. It shows you care about them.

Share Gorilla Stories: Write about why gorillas are important. Explain why we should keep them safe.

Learn and Share: Use books and the internet to find out more about gorillas. Then, share in fun ways, like a project or drawing.

Learn More

Books and Movies: Find books and movies about gorillas.

Online Classes: Take part in online classes or talks to learn from gorilla experts.

Help: You can see gorillas in the wild on tours or volunteer for gorilla projects.

The Quiet Moments: Reflective Solitude in Silverback Life

Silverbacks are the big bosses of gorilla families. They are known for being strong leaders and caring family members. But did you know these mighty gorillas also enjoy their alone time? Let us explore what silverbacks do when they are not busy looking after their troop.

Quiet Time for the Big Boss

Imagine being in charge of a whole family all the time. Sounds exhausting, right? Well, silverback gorillas feel that way too! Sometimes, they need a break from being the leader. During these quiet moments, a silverback might sit alone. He looks at the beautiful forest around him or takes a peaceful nap. This alone time helps him relax. He thinks about the

big and small things he needs to do to keep his family safe and happy.

Why Alone Time is Special

You might have a special place to read, draw, or think. Silverbacks also have their favorite spots in the forest. There, they like to sit quietly. They have this time alone, not because they are sad or lonely. It is because they like the peace and quiet of the jungle. It is their way of taking a deep breath and getting ready for more adventures with their family.

Learning from Quiet Moments

Alone time is not just about sitting around for silverbacks. It is a chance for them to think and learn. They might remember where they found the tastiest fruit or the best place to build a nest. By spending time alone, they are becoming smarter. They are also becoming stronger leaders for their families. Plus, it shows us that everyone needs quiet time, even the strongest and biggest among us. They need it to be their best.

Saying Goodbye to Silverbacks

Remember how strong and smart silverbacks are? They take care of their families and the jungle.

Silverbacks show us how to live together and take care of each other. They are an important part of the jungle.

Let us keep learning about them and help save them. If we all do something, we can make sure gorillas and their jungle homes are safe and happy.

Glossary

- **Silverback Gorillas:** Silverback gorillas are big and strong. They have silver fur on their backs. They are the leaders of their family groups in the jungle.

- **Jungle:** A thick, green forest in warm places where there is always heavy rain fall. It is home to different animals and plants.

- **Troops:** Troops are groups of gorillas. They live together like a family. A silverback gorilla is their leader.

- **Nests:** Beds that gorillas make each night out of leaves and branches to sleep.

- **Leader:** The leader is the head of the gorilla family. They are always silverbacks. They make decisions and keep everyone safe.

- **Body Language:** Body Language is the use of body movements or positions. Gorillas use it to talk to each other without words.

- **Climate:** Climate is the term used to describe the regular patterns of weather. It includes rainfall and temperature in a particular area.

- **Virtual Safari:** Virtual Safari means using the internet to watch videos. You can also use virtual reality to see gorillas in their natural homes from far away. It is like taking a trip to see the gorillas without traveling.

- **Conservation:** It is when we work to keep animals and their homes safe.

Chapter 3: The Emperor's Sacrifice: The Tale of the Antarctic Fathers

The Emperor Penguin Fathers

Ice World Giants

Emperor penguins are the tallest penguins. They have black, white, and yellow feathers. They live in Antarctica, the coldest place on Earth.

Antarctic Dads

In the dark, icy Antarctic, they keep their eggs warm against the freezing wind. Their dedication never wavers. It shows their strength and deep bond with their future offspring. They make every sacrifice to ensure their survival. This is a story about their love and warmth in the chilly world. Even in the coldest place on Earth. These penguin dads show that care and teamwork can create a warm nest of hope for the new generation.

The Penguin Love Song

Singing in the Snow

Emperor Penguins sing in Antarctica to find a partner. Their dance in the snow helps them find a mate for the winter.

Dancing Dads

Singing is not the only thing the penguins do. Their dance helps them find a perfect partner for the winter.

Pairing Up

When two penguins find each other, they touch and groom each other to get closer. You can find love in the cold because they get ready for winter together.

The Long Winter Watch

Sunset and Sacrifice

As winter comes, and the sun sets, penguin dads take over. They hold the eggs on their feet, keeping them warm.

Staying Warm Together

The dads huddle together in the bitter cold. They fast and share warmth. They shield their eggs. The weather is harsh and Antarctic.

The Emperor Penguin Dads' Watch

Staying Strong in the Cold

In Antarctica, dads stand like guards. They warm their eggs without eating to show their strength.

Taking Turns in the Cold

The dads take turns facing the freezing wind to keep the eggs safe. They show they care for the chicks' safety.

Dads Keeping Warm

Dark Days and Warm Hearts

Antarctica is always dark. Father penguins tend to their eggs to keep them warm. They stand with the eggs on their feet, tucked in warm skin.

Love That Doesn't Give Up

No matter how cold or dark it gets, these penguin dads do not stop caring. Their love keeps them going until the eggs hatch, bringing light to the dark winter.

Dads Facing Challenges

Tough Times for Penguin Dads

Penguin dads must learn how to survive world of Antarctica. They watch out for danger and stay strong during storms.

All for Their Chicks

The dads stand close to protect each other and their eggs. They go a long time without food, all to make sure their babies will be born. This shows how brave and loving penguin dads are. They make sure their families stay safe.

Penguin Families in the Antarctic

The Big Thaw

When winter ends, the Emperor Penguin dads see their eggs hatch. The ice echoes with tiny peeps as dads meet their chicks. Moms return to feed. They also celebrate surviving winter.

Growing Together

Life in the ice is tough, but the chicks grow with their parents' help. They learn about life in the cold, getting ready for their future.

Passing on Wisdom

Dads teach their chicks to walk, find shelter, and swim. Their lessons help the chicks get strong. Over time, chicks grow up, but they remember their dads' lessons to stay safe in the cold.

A Call for Penguin Protection

Penguins at Risk

The home of Emperor Penguins is changing. This is because the Earth is getting warmer. This makes life hard for them.

Helping Hand

We can all help save them. Scientists want safe places for penguins. Countries are trying to keep Earth cool. Telling people about penguins can save them. And, helping nature can save them.

Our Part

By caring and helping, we can make a difference. Let us learn and act to protect these wonderful penguins and their icy homes.

Helping the Penguins

Penguins Need Our Help

Emperor Penguins are struggling. Their icy world is getting warmer. This means it is harder for them to find food and safe places to live.

Working Together

Things can get better if we all work together. Scientists want to keep the penguins' home safe. A lot of people are working to keep the world from getting too hot. We can protect penguins if we talk about them and do things that are good for nature.

A Promise to Help

We can all help the Emperor Penguins. These beautiful birds will be around for a long time if we learn about them. And if we care about the earth and do things to help.

Penguin Dads' Brave Story

Ice Heroes

Emperor Penguin dads are super dads. They stand in the deep freeze to keep their babies warm. They show us how much parents will do for their children, even in the wild.

Learning from Penguins

Our story about these dads is finishing. We have seen how brave they are. They teach us to keep trying, to care for our families, and to take care of the Earth. By helping, we make sure these wonderful penguins stay around for a long time.

Glossary

- **Emperor Penguins** are the tallest penguins. They live in the coldest part of the world: Antarctica.

- **Antarctica:** A very cold place at the bottom of the Earth, covered in ice and snow.

- **Grooming** is when penguins clean their own feathers or each other's.

- **Huddle:** When the penguins get close together to share warmth.

- **Fasting:** Going without food for a period.

- **Mating Dance:** Penguins do a mating dance. They do it to show they are ready to be parents and find a partner.

- **Thaw:** When ice and snow melt, usually when it gets warmer after winter.

- **Habitat:** The natural home of an animal or plant.

- **Resilience:** Being strong and able to manage tough times.

Chapter 4: Ospreys – Guardians of the Nest

Ospreys - The Sky's Fishermen

Meet the Ospreys

Imagine a bird that can fly so high and dive straight down super-fast to catch a fish!

That is an osprey, a bird that is good at flying and fishing. They have big wings to glide on the wind and super sharp eyes to spot fish in the water. Their talons are unique. They enable the birds to capture their aquatic prey with great accuracy.

Fishing Like a Pro

Ospreys are famous for catching lots of fish. They float in the air, then zoom down into the water to grab a fish with their strong claws. That is their special talent, and they are impressive at it.

Looking Cool

Ospreys look neat with a mask-like stripe over their eyes and brown and white feathers. Plus, they have cool feet that help them hold on to slippery fish. They are like the top fish-catching birds out there!

Osprey Adventures

We are going to learn all about ospreys, from how they catch their fish to the way they take care of their chicks. Are you ready to fly high with the ospreys? Let us go!

Building a Home in the Sky

Flying Friends

Ospreys team up in pairs, like friends who share everything. They even fly super far together every year to get back to their favorite spot to build a nest.

Their Special Spot

Every year, ospreys come back to the same place to make their home. They pick somewhere high, like on a pole or in a tree, and build a big nest out of sticks.

Making the Nest

Both the mom and dad osprey help make the nest. They find sticks and put them together right, getting ready to welcome their baby ospreys.

The Osprey Dad

More Than a Hunter

Osprey dads do a lot more than catch fish. They help keep the nest safe and warm, and they share all the work with the mom.

Learning to Fish

When the baby ospreys get bigger, the dad teaches them how to fish. He shows them how to soar, dive, and catch their own fish.

Guarding the Nest

Osprey dads are also great at keeping a lookout for danger. They watch over the nest and make sure no other animals come too close to their chicks.

Osprey Chicks Learn to Fly

Flying Lessons

When osprey chicks are ready to fly, their dad becomes their teacher. He shows them how to flap their wings and glide in the sky. With his help, they learn to soar and catch their own fish.

Life After the Nest

Even after the chicks leave the nest, their dad keeps teaching them. He shows them how to be strong and smart in the wild. His lessons help them as they grow up and make their own way.

Dad's Lasting Lessons

The father osprey's hard work makes sure his chicks do well in nature. His care and teaching leave a mark on them for their whole lives.

Dangers in the Wild

Staying Safe

Osprey dads must watch out for dangers like other animals that might try to hurt their chicks. They stay alert to keep their family safe.

Humans and Nature

Sometimes, people can make life hard for ospreys, like when they pollute the water or take down trees. Osprey dads work hard to find safe places for their families to live and find clean food.

Brave Dads

Osprey dads are strong and do not give up, no matter what. They do everything they can to keep their chicks healthy and safe.

Learning from Ospreys

Family First

Osprey dads show us how important families are. They stick together, help each other, and face tough times as a team.

Never Give Up

Osprey dads are tough. They teach us to keep trying, even when things get hard. They find ways to get through problems and keep their families safe.

Birds and the World

A bald eagle can help us remember that everything in nature is connected. They help us understand why we need to look after the world and all the living things that live in it.

Young Bird Fans

Bird Adventures

Osprey dads are perfect for kids to learn about birds. Watching ospreys can teach kids about how birds live and why they are special.

Getting Outside

Birdwatching is a fun way for kids to learn about nature. It helps them love the outdoors and want to take care of it.

Kids Can Help Too

Kids can learn about birds and even help scientists. By joining in, they can make a big difference for birds and the places they live.

Learning More About Ospreys

Books and Films

If you want to learn even more about ospreys, there are lots of books and movies out there. They can tell you about how ospreys live, fly, and take care of their chicks. You can find stories about ospreys in libraries or watch movies about them.

Websites and Helping Out

You can also look up ospreys on the internet. Some websites let you watch ospreys live on camera nests. And if you want to help ospreys, you can join groups that work to keep them safe and their homes clean.

Celebrating Osprey Dads

Osprey Dads Are

Impressive

Osprey dads are cool. They catch lots of fish, protect their chicks, and teach them everything they need to know. They show us how all creatures are connected and why we should take care of our planet.

Learning from Ospreys

Osprey dads can teach us a lot. They deal with tough times and keep their families safe. Their hard work helps us remember to look after the places where animals live.

A Big Thank You

We should thank the Osprey dads for showing us how to be strong and kind. Let us promise to take care of the rivers, lakes, and skies where they live. That way, we help not just ospreys but all living things, including ourselves.

Glossary

- **Osprey:** A large bird that eats fish and can dive into water.

- **Nest:** A home that birds build to lay eggs and take care of their babies.

- **Migration:** When birds travel long distances to find warmer places or more food.

- **Predator:** An animal that hunts and eats other animals for food.

- **Habitat:** The natural home of plants and animals, like forests or lakes.

- **Pollution:** Harmful things that make the air, water, or ground dirty.

- **Talons:** The sharp claws that birds like ospreys use to catch fish.

- **Endangered:** Animals or plants that are at risk of disappearing from our planet.

- **Biodiversity:** Biodiversity is the variety of life found on Earth. It includes all animals, plants, and other living things.

- **Adaptation:** Animals rely on skills or body parts to survive in their habitats. For ospreys, it is their sharp eyes to see fish in the water.

- **Territory:** An area that an animal, like an osprey, claims as its own and defends against others.

- **Incubation:** The process of keeping eggs warm until they hatch into baby birds. Osprey parents take turns doing this.

Chapter 5: Alligators: The Swamp Heroes

Meeting the Alligators

In the southeastern U.S., huge alligators live in swamps.

These alligators have been there for millions of years! Swamps are important. They help alligators and many other animals live together, like in an enormous home. You can find fish, birds, and sometimes even the rare Florida panther. Swamps are special places that help clean water and give animals a safe place to live. It's cool how swamps are like cities for animals!

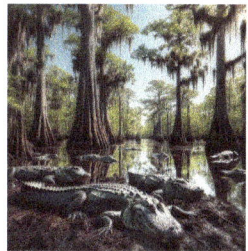

Alligators as Dads

You might not know this, but alligator dads are good at taking care of their babies. Even though they are big and tough, they are also very loving parents.

Swamp Helpers

Alligator dads are like the swamp's care-takers. They keep their home in balance by making sure everything is equal. It is good for your health. They make the plants grow well and keep the swamp looking nice. These animals play a big part in the swamp's life.

Growing Up Alligator

Baby to Leader

Imagine being a tiny alligator in a huge swamp. As they grow, they learn to be strong and eventually become leaders. It is hard, but they do it.

Dads Keeping Watch

When it is time for eggs, alligator dads protect the nest. They make sure it is safe from danger. Their family is of utmost importance to them.

Alligator Dads and Their Nests

Building a Home

Alligator dads help make nests out of plants and mud. They pick a safe spot near water to keep the eggs warm and safe from enemies.

On the Lookout

Fathers stay close to protect the eggs. They make sure the eggs stay safe until they hatch, ready to protect their little ones.

The Truth About Alligator Dads

Changing Minds

Alligator dads care more than you might think. They surprise people by how they look after their nests and eggs.

Learning from Alligators

Alligator dads teach us. They show that scary animals can be gentle with their babies. It makes us rethink what we know about reptiles and find surprises in nature.

Alligator Dads: Swamp Heroes

Nest Protectors

Alligator dads are like heroes, keeping their eggs safe. They watch over their nests, making sure no harm comes to their future babies.

Facing Hard Times

Being an alligator dad is full of challenges. Still, they stay strong. They do it to protect their babies. They keep them safe no matter what.

Tutoring the Babies

Alligator dads stick around to tutor their babies. They show them key skills. For example, swimming and hunting. This helps the babies survive in the wild.

A New Beginning

First Swim

When baby alligators hatch, their dad leads them to the water, making sure they are safe. It is their first big adventure as a family.

Growing as a Family

These first moments in the water are special. They learn to stick together and support each other. They face whatever the swamp throws at them.

Thriving Together

Teamwork Wins

Alligator parents show the power of teamwork. They build nests. They also teach hunting. They give their babies a strong start.

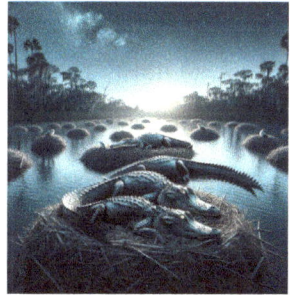

Adapting to the Swamp

Even with dangers, alligators are great at adapting to them. They teach their young how to live well in the swamp, no matter what changes.

Overcoming Nature's Challenges

Surviving Together

Alligators must deal with predators. They also face changes in their environment. But they are tough, protecting their land and babies.

Dealing with People

People cause problems too. They destroy homes and pollute. But there's hope, as people are also trying to help alligators live better.

Lessons from Alligator Dads

Unexpected Teachers

Alligator dads make us see reptile parenting in a new light. They work hard and change our views on caring for their babies.

Seeing Nature Anew

Their efforts make us look at the natural world differently. We learn that all animals have feelings and can work together.

Kids Helping Nature

Exploring the Wild

When kids learn about nature, they start to care about protecting it. They see the importance of alligators. They see it to their environment.

Acting

Teaching kids to help nature shows them what they can do. They can clean up local areas. Or they can support wildlife groups.

Digging Deeper

Learning More

We can tell people where to learn more about alligators. They can watch shows or visit websites. This helps everyone care more.

Helping Out

We encourage people to help nature. Small actions can make a big difference. They protect alligators and their homes.

Reptile World Examples

More Than Survival

Alligator dads do more than protect. They nurture and teach. They make sure their home thrives.

A Call to Care

Their story reminds us to protect all kinds of life. It is important for everyone to help keep our world diverse and alive.

Glossary

- **Alligators:** Big lizards with strong mouths. They live in wetlands in the southeast part of the USA. They can be a bit scary but are very interesting.

- **Swamps:** Places with a lot of water, plants, and trees. Alligators and many other animals live there.

- **Caretakers:** People or animals that take care of others. Alligator dads take care of the swamp like it is their big garden.

- **Balance:** Making sure everything is right, not too much and not too little. In the swamp, it means having the right number of animals and plants.

- **Nest:** A safe spot where animals put their eggs. Alligator dads use mud and plants to make nests to keep the eggs safe.

- **Protect:** To protect means to ensure the safety of someone or something. Alligator dads watch over their nests to keep danger away.

- **Leaders:** Someone who shows others the way. Big alligators are like the bosses of the swamp.

- **Challenges:** Tough things that need to be fixed or dealt with. Alligator dads have to deal with dangers and changes in their home.

- **Adapt:** Changing how you do things to fit in with new situations. Alligators are really good at getting used to changes in their swamp.

- **Predators:** Predators hunt other animals for food. Alligator dads must keep their babies safe. They must keep them safe from these hunters.

- **Teamwork** means working together. It is done as a group to achieve something.

- **Nurture:** Helping someone to grow up strong and healthy. Alligator dads teach their babies how to swim and find food.

- **Diversity:** Having lots of various kinds of things or people. The alligators show us the many animals and plants in the swamp.

- **Habitat:** The natural home of an animal or plant.

Chapter 6: Arctic Wolves – Masters of Survival and Teaching

Arctic Wolves: Masters of the Ice

White Wanderers

Imagine a wolf family, white as snow, living in the vast Arctic.

They are not surviving; they are thriving. With their thick fur, they hunt and roam, teaching their little ones how to make it in the cold.

Working Together

The wolves win against the Arctic chill. They do it by sticking together. Dad wolves are key. They teach their pups survival secrets. They cover finding food and staying safe. It is their teamwork that makes them strong in the icy wild.

Family Life in the Arctic

Frost-bound

Deep in the Arctic, wolf families form a close unit. Every wolf has a caring dad. Each plays a part in the family's life. They make sure they all stay safe and fed in the snow.

Learning to Thrive

In the pack, every day is a lesson in survival. The older wolves teach the young ones all they need to know. They teach them from hunting to how to be part of the pack. This way, the pack grows strong, ready to face the Arctic together.

Nurturing Arctic Wolf Dads

Caring Leaders

Arctic wolf dads show a softer side, helping raise their pups with love. They play, protect, and teach. They keep their family close and strong.

Teaching How to Thrive

They teach their pups to hunt and communicate, readying them for life in the Arctic. These lessons are key to their pack's success.

The Arctic Hunt Together

Hunting as a Team

Wolf dads lead their family in hunting, using smart teamwork to find food in the snow. This teamwork is vital for their survival.

Feasting Together

When they catch their prey, the entire pack shares the meal. This sharing helps keep everyone fed. It also strengthens their bond.

Winning Against the Cold

The Arctic Test

Arctic wolves live in a world of ice, fighting every day to survive. Their teamwork and smart plans, led by the dad wolves, help them win this icy battle.

Sticking Together

What keeps them going is how tight they are as a group. Smart dad wolves guide them. The pack faces the unwelcoming world together. This teamwork shows they can beat even the toughest ice.

Arctic wolves live in a world that is ever-changing.

A Transforming Arctic

The Arctic is shifting, changing how and where Arctic wolves live. With ice melting and the land changing, finding food and a place to call home gets tougher.

New Ways to Hunt

It is getting harder to find the animals they usually hunt. So, Arctic wolves are figuring out new ways to hunt. They track animals. They search for fresh places in their changing world. This cleverness helps them find enough food. It keeps their packs healthy.

Closer Together

Their world is changing. Arctic wolf packs are growing even closer. They stick together. They face new lands and challenges as one. This teamwork makes them even stronger, helping them do well in a world that is warming up.

Wolf Dads of the Arctic

Caring Protectors

Arctic wolf dads do more than watch over their young; they care for and teach them. This helps their family survive. It also helps them grow strong together.

Teaching Survival

With patience, these dads teach their pups how to live in the icy world. They pass on important skills so the pack can stick together and thrive.

Encouraging Young Explorers

Discover the Arctic

Let us learn about the Arctic and help keep it safe. By exploring this unique place, we can protect its animals and ice.

Learn and Help

Check out books and websites about Arctic wolves. Join conservation groups. They protect wolves and their habitat.

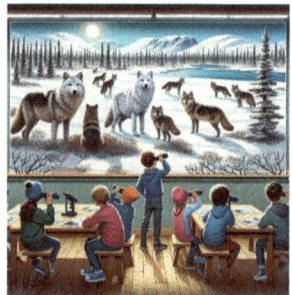

Celebrating Arctic Wolf Dads

Heroes of the Ice

Arctic wolf dads are the heroes of the snowy world, showing us how to be strong and caring. They teach their families to survive in the cold and keep the balance of nature.

Lessons of Love and Leadership

Wolf dads teach us important lessons. They teach about caring and teamwork. They show that even the toughest animals have a soft side. They care for their families.

Taking Care of Their House

We should take care of the Arctic and its animals because of their story. Protecting their environment is key. It ensures the future of these amazing wolf families.

A Call to Care

Let us learn from Arctic wolf dads to care for and protect our planet. Their lives remind us to be kind to all creatures. They also remind us to work together for a better world.

Glossary

- **Arctic Wolves:** Large, white wolves that live in the Arctic. They have thick fur to keep them warm and are great at living in the cold.

- **Surviving** means staying alive. This is especially true in tough conditions, like the cold Arctic.

- **Thriving:** Doing well and being healthy, not getting by.

- **Pack:** A family of wolves that live, hunt, and do everything together.

- **Hunting** is looking for and catching food. It is like how wolves find and catch animals to eat.

- **Feasting** means eating lots of food. It is usually in a group.

- **The Arctic is transforming**. Ice is melting and landscapes are shifting.

- **Adapting:** Changing or adjusting to new conditions.

- **Conservation:** It means protecting nature. It also means caring for animals.

- **Ecosystem:** It is a community of living things, like plants and animals. They work with their environment.

- **Climate change** causes weather changes. For example, it causes the world to get warmer. This warming can melt

Arctic ice.

- **Prey:** Prey refers to animals that other animals hunt and eat.

- **Patience:** Being able to wait, even if it takes a long time or is difficult.

- **Communication:** Sharing or exchanging information. Wolves use sounds and body language to talk to each other.

- **Leadership** means leading or guiding others. It is like how dad wolves lead their packs.

- **Bond:** It is a close connection between individuals.

- **Nurturing** is caring for. It is also about encouraging growth

Chapter 7: The Red Fox – A Father's Care in Nature

Red Fox Families

Meet the Red Fox: A Clever Wild Animal

Watching red fox families is fascinating.

They do many cool things together and can live anywhere. Red foxes are not picky eaters at all—they munch on little animals and even snack on berries and apples. The mom and dad foxes are excellent teachers to their baby foxes, called kits. They show them how to find food and be sneaky hunters. Red foxes are very smart. They handle

change well and care for their families. This makes them great animals to learn about.

The Red Fox Family: Loving and Close

In a cozy spot in the woods, a red fox family stays warm together. The father fox has fur like the sunset. He looks after his family with love as bright as his color.

The Father Red Fox

Dads Work Hard: Before the Kits Come

At night, the father fox is busy bringing food and helping his mate. He makes sure she has everything she needs, showing his love and care.

New Beginnings: The Kits Are Here

In their quiet home, the father fox greets his new babies with gentle touches. He is proud and full of love for each little one.

Teaching and Caring: What Fathers Do

When the sun comes up, the father fox takes his kits out to learn about life. He teaches them how to hunt and stay safe with kindness and wisdom.

Big Brother and Sisters Help Too: Teamwork in the Family

Older brothers and sisters help their parents. They do this by teaching their new kits. They show them how to live in the woods, making the family even stronger.

Wildlife Challenges

The Wild Can Be Hard: Red Foxes Stay Strong

Life outside has dangers. Other animals might hurt them, and winters are cold. But the Red Fox family stays together and is strong, even when times are hard.

Fathers Keep Watch: They Protect the Family

The father fox is always ready to protect his family. He is like a brave guard, making sure everyone is safe.

Learning and Playing

Learning to Hunt: It is Important for Living

The father fox teaches his kits to hunt. These skills are important for them to live in the wild.

Fun and Games: Playing Helps Kits Learn

The Red Fox family plays together. Through playing, they learn key lessons. They grow closer and learn how to work as a team.

Nature and Helping Foxes

People and Nature: How We Can Help Foxes

People can sometimes hurt the places where red foxes live. But we can also help by taking care of nature and keeping their homes safe.

Everyone Can Help: Caring for Fox Homes

We can all do things to help red foxes. Planting trees and cleaning up the woods are great ways to be effective.

Cultural Significance: Foxes in Folklore

Foxes in Stories: Cunning and Clever

From ancient tales to modern fables, the red fox prances through stories across the world. They remind us of the wisdom in nature and the importance of listening to the earth's stories.

Interactive Elements for Young Explorers

Be a Fox for a Day

Activity: Imagine you are a red fox. What would you do? Where would you explore? Draw a picture of your adventure in the wild or in the city. Remember, red foxes are clever and curious!

Fox Detective

Activity: Go on a "fox hunt" in your neighborhood or local park (no real foxes involved!). Look for signs that a fox might be around, like tracks or food remains. Take photos or make drawings of what you find.

Fox Home Builder

Activity: Build a mini fox den with sticks and leaves. Create a cozy and safe environment, like a fox.

Storytime with Foxes

Activity: Create your own short story or comic strip about a day in the life of a red fox family. What challenges do they face? How do they work together to overcome them?

Fox Conservation Hero

Activity: Learn about one way people are helping protect red foxes and their habitats. Then, draw a poster that shows how you can be a hero for foxes, too. Share your poster with friends or family to spread the word about fox conservation.

Fox Facts Quiz

Activity: Make a fun quiz with interesting facts about red foxes. Quiz your family or friends to see who knows the most about these fascinating creatures!

Connect with Nature

Activity: Observe and learn about red foxes at a wildlife sanctuary or park.

Conclusion: Celebrating Red Fox Fathers

Red Fox Fathers: Kind and Brave

Red fox fathers are great teachers. They show us how to love and be kind. Let us honor these amazing animals and help protect their homes.

A Call to Care

Red foxes teach us to care for nature. When we care for them, we are also taking care of our world. Let us make sure the red fox fathers can keep being a symbol of love in nature.

Glossary

- **Red Foxes:** These are wild animals that look a bit like dogs and have beautiful, bright red fur. They are very clever and can live in lots of various places, from woods to city streets.

- **Adaptation:** This is when animals change a little bit to make sure they can live in their homes. Red foxes do this well because they can make a home in both quiet forests and busy cities.

- **Habitat:** This is where animals or plants live and grow. Red foxes can have their habitat in lots of places, like in a green forest or even in a park in the middle of a city.

- **Kits:** These are what we call baby red foxes. They stay with their mom and dad who look after them until they are big enough to take care of themselves.

- **Monogamous:** Animals that stay together for life. Red foxes are an example of monogamous animals.

- **Den:** This is a comfortable and safe place where red foxes live. It is where they sleep, relax, and where they look after their cute little kits.

- **Prey:** These are the animals that red foxes hunt to eat, like bunnies and birds.

- **Survival Skills:** Animals need to know survival skills to find food and stay safe.

- **Cunning:** This word means being smart and good at figuring things out. Red foxes are cunning due to their problem-solving abilities and survival skills.

- **Urbanization:** Urbanization is the act of building new cities and towns.

- **Predator:** These are animals that hunt other animals for food. Red foxes are predators because they hunt smaller animals.

Part II

Northern Cardinals, Marmoset Monkeys, Bald Eagles, Spotted Hyenas, Maned Wolves, Bearded Dragons, and Grevy's Zebras

Chapter 8: Northern Cardinals – Caring Dads of the Bird World

Discover the Northern Cardinals

Bright Red Birds

Meet the Northern Cardinals. They have dazzling red feathers and pointy crests.

Their bright colors make them stand out wherever they are. These bright birds often add color to backyards. This is especially true in the winter against the white snow.

Caring Fathers

Did you know? Male cardinals are amazing dads. Unlike many birds, where mom does most of the work, cardinal dads help a lot with their babies. They feed their females during courtship. They take turns warming the eggs. This shows their commitment to family care.

Cardinals in Your Garden

Faithful Companions

Cardinals are loyal friends. They pick one partner and stay together all year long, showing us what true loyalty looks like.

Working as a Team

Building a home and taking care of babies is teamwork for cardinals. They share the job of keeping the eggs warm and then both feed their chicks until they are ready to fly.

Building a Nest

Using twigs, leaves, and grass, cardinals make a cozy nest. They hide it in bushes or trees to protect their family.

The Parenting Journey

Taking Turns with the Eggs

Both mom and dad cardinal take turns sitting on their nest. They have two to five eggs. They ensure the eggs are always warm and safe.

Feeding the Mother Bird

While mom sits on the eggs, dad goes out to find food, bringing it back to show his care and support.

Feeding the Chicks

Once the chicks hatch, dad continues to bring food, teaching them how to eat until they can find food on their own.

Equal Duties

They build nests, warm eggs, and feed chicks. Cardinal dads do as much as moms. They make sure their little ones grow up strong and safe.

Daily Life of Cardinal Families

Finding Food

Every day is a hunt for food as dad cardinal searches for insects, seeds, and berries to feed his family.

Guarding the Nest

Always on the lookout, dad cardinal protects his nest from any danger, keeping his family safe.

Choosing the Right Food

Choosing the best food is crucial. Dad cardinal knows exactly what to bring back to keep everyone healthy and strong.

The Cardinal Way

Caring for Each Other

By sharing the work, cardinal parents create a loving home. They also create a supportive one for their chicks.

Helping the Chicks Grow

Even after the chicks leave the nest, their dad continues to look after them. He teaches them about the world.

Strong Family Ties

Cardinal fathers' dedication strengthens the family bond. It makes sure the young feel loved and secure.

Staying Safe

From cats to snakes and large birds, many dangers threaten cardinal families. They stay vigilant to keep everyone safe.

Challenges and Conservation

Changes in Their Home

Our changing world has more cities, farms, and climate shifts. This poses big challenges for cardinals. They struggle to find food and safe places to live.

The Importance of Green Spaces

As we build more buildings and roads, we take the homes of many birds. This includes the Northern Cardinals. Green spaces, such as parks, gardens, and forests, are essential. Birds need them to find food, shelter, and mates. These areas give cardinals a place to live, away from the hustle and bustle of city life.

Northern Cardinal Fathers: A Lesson in Commitment

True Commitment

Northern Cardinal dads show us what hard work and love look like. They remind us to be responsible and committed to those we care about.

Wonders of Nature

These beautiful birds do more than just look pretty. They help nature by spreading seeds and keeping insect populations in check.

Inspiring a Love for Birds

Encouraging Curiosity

Let us encourage kids to learn about birds like the Northern Cardinals. Asking questions and observing nature can spark a lifelong interest.

The Joy of Bird Watching

Bird watching is a fun way to connect with nature. It teaches us about different birds and the importance of protecting their habitats.

Learn More About Northern Cardinals

Educational Resources

There are many books, websites, and groups dedicated to teaching about Northern Cardinals. These resources are full of interesting facts and stories.

Groups Who Protect Birds

Learn about organizations that work to protect birds and their environments. Find out how you can help keep birds like the Northern Cardinals safe for future generations.

Celebrating Cardinal Fathers

Bright and Loving

Let us celebrate the male Northern Cardinal. It has striking red feathers. They are a symbol of his love and dedication to his family.

Beyond Beauty

These birds remind us that beauty is not just about looks. Male cardinals are also incredible fathers, a fact that might surprise many.

Learning from Cardinals

They teach us valuable lessons. These can apply to everyone. The lessons are about teamwork, perseverance, and dedication.

Caring for Our World

Admiring these birds is just the start. We should also work to protect them and their habitats because they play a vital role in our ecosystem.

A Thanks to Cardinal Fathers

Thank you to the Northern Cardinal dads. They are caring parents and add a lot to the bird world.

Glossary

- **Crest:** A tuft of feathers on the top of a bird's head that it can raise or lower. Northern Cardinals have crests, which make them easily recognizable.

- **Foraging:** The act of searching for food. Northern Cardinals forage for seeds. They also eat insects and berries. They do this to feed themselves and their chicks.

- **Incubation** is keeping eggs warm. It continues until they hatch. Male and female Northern Cardinals take turns. They both incubate their eggs.

- **Monogamous:** Having one mate for a period of time or for life. Cardinals are monogamous. They often stay with the same partner.

- **Nest:** A structure that birds build to lay their eggs and raise their young. Cardinals build nests out of twigs, leaves, and grass.

- **Plumage:** The feathers covering a bird's body. Male Northern Cardinals have bright red feathers.

- **Urbanization** is the development of land for cities and towns. It often leads to the loss of natural habitats for wildlife.

- **Conservation:** The protection and preservation of nature and wildlife.

- **Habitat:** The natural home or environment of an animal, plant, or other organism. Northern Cardinals live in forests, gardens, and green spaces.

- **Migrate:** To move from one region or habitat to another, often seasonally. Northern Cardinals are non-migratory, meaning they stay in their home range year-round.

- **Seed Dispersal:** The movement or transport of seeds away from the parent plant. Northern Cardinals help in seed dispersal. They do this by eating fruits and seeds and then excreting them in various places.

Chapter 9: Marmoset Monkeys – Little Heroes of the Jungle

Introduction

Welcome to the world of marmoset monkeys!

Meet the marmoset monkeys, tiny jungle wonders with big personalities.

Imagine living in a world filled with the sounds of chattering. You would also hear the rustling of leaves as these small monkeys leap from tree to tree. Marmosets are not much bigger than squirrels. But they are full of energy and have sharp eyes that miss nothing. They live in the lush, green forests close to the equator,

where it is warm and rains a lot. These forests are their playgrounds, full of adventures and secrets.

Marmoset Habitats

Where Marmosets Live

Marmoset monkeys can live in many places. They can be found in the thick rainforests of South America and even in cities! They are good at living in various places, but we need to keep their homes safe.

Marmoset Family Life

The Importance of Fathers

In marmoset families, fathers are important. They help a lot with the babies, keeping them safe and caring for them. This helps make a strong family and keeps the little ones safe in the big jungle.

Different Monkey Families

Other monkeys, like chimpanzees and gorillas, also care for their families. But, they do so in different ways. Some babies are mostly looked after by their mothers, but marmosets share the job. This helps us learn how different animals take care of their families.

Working Together to Raise Babies

Marmosets are known for sticking together like a team. In their families, everyone has a role to play, from finding food to watching out for danger. What makes them special is how they all pitch in to care for the babies. It is not just a job for mom; dad and even siblings join in. This way, each baby marmoset gets lots of attention. They learn all they need to know about jungle life.

Dads Are Special

Dads and their Bonding Time

Male marmosets are great dads. They carry their babies around and keep them close. This makes the babies feel safe and loved. We can see these sweet moments when the dads take their babies through the trees.

Cleaning and Playing

Marmoset dads also clean their babies and play with them. It is not just for staying clean. It is also for building strong family ties and teaching the babies how to be good monkeys.

Feeding the Little Ones

Dads also help find food for the babies, like bugs and fruits. They make sure their babies eat well to grow up strong. This shows how much the dads care about their babies.

Learning About Dad's Important Role

Caring Connections

Marmoset dads show a lot of love to their babies. They groom them, cuddle them, and share sweet moments. These dads show us that animals can have deep feelings, just like people.

Sharing Food

Marmoset dads have an important job in feeding their babies. They share their food carefully to keep their little ones healthy and happy.

Playing and Teaching

Playtime with dad is fun and teaches the babies how to live in the wild. The dads show them how to find food and how to have a good relationship with other monkeys.

Looking Out for Danger

Marmoset parents are always watching out for their babies. They work together to keep them safe and to make a home where they can grow up well.

Benefits of Cooperative Care

The Good Things About Being a Marmoset Parent

Scientists have found that the way marmosets care for their young is good for the marmosets. It keeps the family together and helps the babies stay alive. This family does very well thanks to both moms and dads.

Teamwork in Parenting: Marmoset Monkeys Show Us How

In the world of marmoset monkeys, moms and dads work together to take care of their babies. They help each other out, using each other's strengths. This teamwork helps their little ones grow up safe and healthy.

Teamwork Makes the Family Strong

Marmoset monkeys have a distinct way of living together. They do not just live; they help each other to live better. Moms and dads both do important jobs, like finding food and watching over their babies. Everyone helps, and this makes their family ties strong.

Teamwork helps all the family members to be happy and do well. When they all work together, they can face any challenge.

Facing the World Together

Staying Safe from Danger

Marmoset families must be careful because there are animals in the jungle that can harm them. They must be quick and watchful to keep their little ones safe.

Protecting Their Home

The place where marmosets live is changing. This is because of the weather and what people do, such as cutting down trees. We need to take care of their homes so they can survive.

Conservation and Education

We Can Help Marmosets

We can learn a lot from marmosets about working together and taking care of each other. These lessons can help us be better with our own families and friends.

Keeping Marmosets Safe

We must protect the homes of marmosets and keep them safe. This means we need to take care of the forests and stop harming their homes.

Encouraging Kids to Love Nature

Marmosets are a wonderful way for kids to learn about the amazing things in nature. Kids can explore outside, learn about different animals, and grow to care about our world.

Youth and Conservation

Young People Making a Difference

There are kids just like you who have done wonderful things for the environment. They show that even one person can make a significant difference.

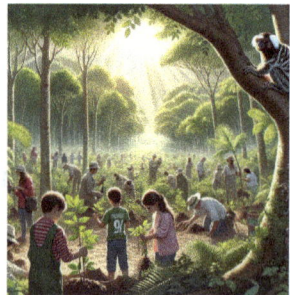

Getting Involved and Learning More

Kids can learn more about marmosets by doing fun things like drawing or researching. Visiting places where animals are taken care of can help kids see why it is important to protect them.

Helping Marmosets

There are groups that work to keep marmoset homes safe. You can join them, help plant trees, or teach others about marmosets.

Conclusion: Honoring Marmoset Dads

Saying Thank You to Marmoset Dads

We say goodbye to the marmoset monkeys, and we thank the dads for taking such loving care of their families. They show us what it means to be a good parent.

We can learn from these dads how to be better people and take care of each other. Let us remember the lessons they teach us about love and looking after our world.

Glossary

- **Marmoset Monkeys** are small and playful. They live in the tropical forests and are known for their close family bonds.

- **Tropical forests** are warm and wet. They are near the equator. Trees grow tall there. Many kinds of plants and animals live there.

- **Unique Traits** are distinctive features or habits. They make someone or something different from others.

- **Cooperative Care** is when family members work together

to care for their babies. They share tasks like feeding and protecting them.

- **Habitats:** The natural homes or environments where animals and plants live.

- **Rainforests:** Dense forests found in tropical areas, with lots of rain, that are home to a huge variety of life.

- **Bonding Time:** These are special moments spent together. They help to build strong love and connection.

- **Groom:** To clean and brush the fur or feathers of another animal.

- **Cuddle:** To hold someone or something close in your arms to show love or affection.

- **Conservation:** The protection and preservation of nature, including plants, animals, and their habitats.

- **Predators:** Animals that hunt other animals for food.

- **Teamwork:** Working together with others towards a common goal or task.

- The **environment** is the natural world. It is where living things, including humans, plants, and animals, exist and interact.

Chapter 10: Bald Eagles – Devoted Dads of the Sky

Introduction: Majestic Bald Eagles

Meet the Bald Eagle. It is a symbol of freedom.

It has a striking white head, sharp eyes, and powerful wings. These great birds soar across the skies of North America. They fly from Alaska's cold lands to Mexico's warm coasts. Guess what? Their eyes are so good at seeing things far away that they can find a fish from a mile away! This helps them catch their food in a perfect dive.

Where Eagles Live

Bald Eagles love places with lots of water. These are places like lakes, rivers, and
coasts. They love them because that is
where they find their favorite food: fish.
They build their huge nests high up in tall
trees or cliffs to keep a sharp eye out for food
and danger.

Eagle Families: Together Forever

Bald Eagles are not just majestic. They are also loving partners and
parents. They pick one mate for life, creating a strong team to build
nests and care for their young.

Building a Home Together

Nest Sweet Nest

Imagine a nest as big as a car; that is what
Bald Eagles build using sticks and branches. Their nests are called eyries. Bald Eagles
place their nests high up to avoid danger
and have a beautiful view of the surroundings.

Eggs and Eaglets

Both mom and dad eagle share the job of keeping their eggs warm until they hatch. They take turns sitting on the nest, always on the lookout to protect their future chicks from harm.

A Team Effort

Eagle parents show how important it is to work together and look out for each other by splitting up their work. They show how balance and unity can make a family stronger. Their actions show how important it is to work together. They show how important it is to help and be careful. It's easy to see how working together can benefit the whole family.

Dad's Hunting Adventures

Feeding the Family

Dad eagle is a great hunter. He dives to catch fish. Or he grabs other small animals to feed his hungry family. He brings the food back to the nest, making sure his chicks have enough to eat and grow strong.

Guardian of the Nest

The father eagle hunts. He also stands
guard, watching over his family. He protects
them from predators. He also shields them
from harsh weather. This makes sure they
are safe and comfortable.

Learning to Fly

First Flight

This is an exciting time for eagle families.
It is when the young eaglets take their first
flight. With their parents' encouragement,
they leap out of the nest. They flap their
wings and start to explore the sky.

Growing Up

The eaglets learn to fly. Their parents keep
watching them. They teach them to hunt
and survive. It is a gradual process of learning, growing, and gaining independence.

The Cycle of Life

A Year in the Life

Bald Eagles' lives are full of interesting events. They build nests and lay eggs. Then, they raise eaglets and teach them to fly. Each year, eagle parents repeat this cycle. They help their species survive.

Protecting Bald Eagles

A Success Story

Bald Eagles were once in danger of disappearing. But people are working together to protect them and their homes. This has caused their numbers to grow. They remind us of the power of conservation and the difference we can make.

Inspiring Young Protectors

Bald Eagles inspire us to care for our planet and its wildlife. By learning more about these birds, and how we can help them, we can all help keep our world beautiful and full of life.

Educational Activities: Discovering Bald Eagles

Eagle Eye View

Activity: Binoculars Craft

Goal: Create a pair of "binoculars" using toilet paper rolls and string. Decorate them with eagle-inspired designs. Then, go on a nature walk to observe birds and nature, pretending to spot bald eagles from afar.

Materials: Toilet paper rolls, string, markers, stickers.

Nest Building Challenge

Activity: Build a Mini Eagle Nest

Goal: Learn about nest building's details. Do this by making a small version using twigs, leaves, and grass. Discuss the importance of nest placement for protection and food access.

Materials: Twigs, leaves, grass, bowl, or shallow container.

Eagle Facts Scavenger Hunt

Activity: Bald Eagle Fact Quest

Goal: Create a scavenger hunt with facts about bald eagles. Hide these facts around your home or classroom and let kids find them. Each fact can lead to the next through a clue or riddle.

Materials: Paper, markers, facts about bald eagles.

Artistic Feathers

Activity: Feather Art

Goal: Explore the importance of feathers. They are for flight and insulation for bald eagles. Create feather art by painting feather shapes. Or use real feathers to make bald eagle art.

Materials: Paper, paint, brushes, feathers (optional).

Eagle Conservation Poster

Activity: Protect the Eagles Poster

Goal: Discuss the importance of conservation. Explain how everyone can help protect bald eagles. Make posters to raise awareness. They will be on protecting bald eagles and their homes.

Materials: Poster board, markers, crayons, eco-friendly glitter.

Virtual Eagle Watching

Activity: Online Eagle Nest Cam Viewing

Goal: Watch a live feed of a bald eagle nest to observe the daily activities of these majestic birds. Discuss the observations. This includes parenting, feeding, and chick growth.

Materials: Computer or tablet with internet access.

Eagle-inspired Storytime

Activity: Write an Eagle Adventure Story

Goal: Encourage creativity and storytelling. Do this by writing short stories or making comic strips. They should be about the adventures of a bald eagle family. Focus on the challenges and triumphs of the eagle parents and their eaglets.

Materials: Paper, pencils, colored pencils, or markers.

Diet of an Eagle

Activity: What is for dinner?

Goal: Understand the diet of a bald eagle through an interactive matching game. Match pictures of fish, small mammals, and other prey to the bald eagle. Discuss the importance of a healthy ecosystem for food sources.

Materials: Printed or drawn pictures of eagles and their prey, glue, cardboard.

Conclusion: Skyward Bound

Bald Eagle dads show us the importance of care, courage, and commitment. They are not just powerful birds. They are also devoted fathers. They play a key role in their families and the environment. Let us celebrate these amazing dads of the sky. And let us remember to protect our feathered friends and their homes.

Glossary

- The **Bald Eagle** is a large bird of prey. It has a white head and tail. It is known for its strength and beauty. It lives in North America.

- **Symbol of Freedom:** Something that represents or stands for the idea of being free.

- **Prey:** Animals that are hunted and eaten by other animals.

- **Dive:** A steep descent by a bird toward the ground to catch prey.

- **Nests** are structures built by birds to lay their eggs and raise their young.

- **Eaglets:** Baby eagles.

- **Majestic:** Something unbelievably beautiful, impressive, or dignified.

- **Partners** are two animals that live together and help each other. They are especially a male and a female that mate and raise young.

- **Hunt:** To chase and catch something for food.

- **Predators:** Animals that hunt and eat other animals.

- **Soar:** To fly high in the sky with little effort, often with the wings spread wide.

- **Conservation:** Protecting and preserving natural resources and the environment.

- **Species:** A group of living organisms that are like each other and can breed together.

- An **ecosystem** is a community of living things. It includes their environment and how they interact.

- Binoculars: A tool that makes far away objects look closer and clearer when you look through them.

Chapter 11: Spotted Hyenas – The Unsung Heroes of the Clan

Introduction to Spotted Hyenas

Masters of Adaptation

Step into the world of the spotted hyena, a superb survivor from Africa.

These animals do more than survive. They thrive because they can adjust to many situations and are very smart. Spotted hyenas are more than the tricky scavengers some people think they are. They have a social life that is both interesting and complex.

The Clan's Social Fabric

A Female-Led World

Spotted hyenas stand out in the animal kingdom for their female-led groups. The females aren't just in charge. They're also bigger, stronger, and command more respect than the males. They don't show off. They use their strength to guide and protect the clan through all challenges.

Everyone Has a Role

In the hyena's world, males have their own special roles too. They might not sit at the top of the social ladder, but their contributions are vital. From standing guard to scouting for food, they play a key role in the clan's wellbeing. In the spotted hyena clan, everyone has a status. They come together to support each other. It's the perfect example of teamwork in action.

Raising the Next Generation

Teamwork Makes the Dream Work

In a hyena clan, it is not just about one hyena; it is about all of them. Male hyenas help the strong female leaders and the rest of the clan to take care of the babies. They may not be the main ones to look after the cubs, but they are very important. They play with the cubs and teach them how to find food and stay safe. Male hyenas help make sure the young ones have everything they need to grow up well.

A Village to Raise a Cub

The spotted hyenas have a great way of making sure all their babies are looked after. It does not matter whose baby it is everyone helps. This way, all the cubs have a good chance to grow up strong and healthy. When everyone in the clan helps each other like this, it makes the whole group stronger.

Social Dynamics and Communication

The Language of Laughter

The laughing sounds that hyenas make are not just for fun. They use these sounds to tell each other about who they are, how old they are, and how they are feeling. When a baby hyena makes these sounds, it is learning how to talk to the rest of the clan.

A Dance of Dominance and Submission

Hyenas also talk with their bodies. They show if they are in charge or if they are being respectful by the way they act. The baby hyenas watch and learn from this. They see how to be with others in the clan and how to show if they are strong or if they are listening.

The Survival of the Wisest

For baby hyenas, learning how to talk to the clan is very important. It helps them to call for help and to know where they belong in the clan. They start to learn this when they are very young, and it helps them to grow up confident.

Challenges in the Wild

Life for a male spotted hyena is not easy. They live on the African plains, which can be a tough place. Every day, they have to overcome many problems to survive.

The Struggle for Status and Survival

Male hyenas have to work hard because they are not the leaders of the clan. They often get food last and need to help a lot to keep the clan going. When food and water are hard to find, their job gets even harder.

Climate Change: A Looming Threat

Changes in the weather, like not enough rain or too much rain, make life harder for hyenas. It can change where they live and what they eat. For the males, this means they have to be very good at adapting to new situations.

Engaging Young Readers: Activities and Appreciation

Hyena Role-play Activity

Pretend to be a hyena for a day. Will you be the leader, a good hunter, or a little hyena learning everything? This game helps kids imagine being a hyena and learn about how they work together.

Crafting Corner: Make Your Own Hyena Clan

Make your own hyena crafts at home. You can make masks or even a model of where hyenas live. These projects are fun and help kids learn about hyenas and where they live.

Hyena Conservation Projects

Help keep hyenas safe by making posters about them or joining an "Adopt a Hyena" program. Even small things can help hyenas and the places they live.

Story Time: Legends of the Hyena

Read old stories about hyenas from different places in the world. These stories teach us about respect, being smart, and nature. Talking about these stories helps kids learn about different cultures. They also learn how those cultures see nature.

Conclusion: A Tribute to Hyena Societies

We finish our story about hyenas. They are not just animals in Africa. They have an important part in the story of life. Hyenas live together in big families, just like people do, and each one has a special job to do.

Interdependence in Hyena and Human Societies

Hyenas need each other to live well, just like people need to work together in their communities. This helps everyone do better and be stronger.

Inspiring a Future of Coexistence

Let us learn from hyenas about working to-gether and respecting each other. This will help us take care of nature. By doing this, we respect all life. It helps create a world where people and animals can live together happily. This includes hyenas.

By caring for hyenas, we are also helping all the different kinds of life on Earth. Let us all do our part to keep our planet's wildlife and their homes safe.

Glossary

- **Adaptation:** The way animals change over time to survive better in their homes. Like how spotted hyenas have learned to live in many places and find different kinds of food.

- In a **matriarchal society**, the females (like moms and aunts) are in charge. They make the big decisions.

- A **scavenger** is an animal. It finds and eats leftover food that other animals have left behind. Though people often think hyenas do this, they are also great hunters.

- **Communication:** The ways animals talk to each other using sounds, movements, or smells. Hyenas use special laughs and body language to chat with their clan.

- **Dominance:** When one animal shows it's the boss over oth-ers. In hyena clans, some members are more in charge be-cause of their strength or age.

- **Submission:** When an animal shows it's not looking to fight or be the boss, often to keep peace in the group.

- **Clan:** A big family of hyenas living together, helping each other find food and stay safe.

- **Survivor:** An animal that is really good at staying alive, even when it's tough, like the spotted hyena.

- **Habitat:** The natural home of an animal. Spotted hyenas live in African plains and forests.

- **Ecosystem:** A community of all the living things in an area and how they affect each other and their home. Hyenas are an important part of their ecosystem.

- **Conservation** is working to protect animals, plants, and their homes. The goal is to make sure they are around for a long time.

- **Predator:** An animal that hunts other animals for food. Hyenas are predators, but they also eat leftovers.

- **Cub:** A baby hyena.

- **Role:** The job or part an animal plays in its family or group. Like how male hyenas help take care of the babies.

- **Climate Change** refers to changes in the world's weather. These changes can make it harder for animals to find food and a safe place to live. It affects where hyenas can live and what they can eat.

Chapter 12: Maned Wolves – Guardians of the Grasslands

Introduction to Maned Wolves

Mysterious Canids of South America

Imagine you are walking across big, open fields in South America.

Out of nowhere, you see an amazing animal far away. The animal stands tall, boasting a red-brown coat, long legs, and a mane that moves in the wind. This cool animal is the maned wolf. It looks like a fox but stands tall like a deer.

Solitary Yet Social

Even though maned wolves like to be alone, they find friends when it is time to have babies. They have a special way of showing love when they choose a partner. Once they find a mate, they stay together and take turns looking after their little ones. This shows us that even animals that spend a lot of time alone can have strong family ties.

The Whisper of the Grasslands

Maned wolves have a unique way of talking to each other across the big fields. They make a sound like a sad musical instrument that can be heard far away. This sound lets them talk to each other even when they cannot see one another.

Understanding Maned Wolf Societies

Life in the Grasslands and Forests

The maned wolf lives in various places, like open fields with tall grass and forests with lots of trees. They are exceptionally good at living in these places and know how to find food in both the grass and the woods. They can be quiet and sneaky when they need to be.

The Family Unit

Maned wolves find one partner and stay with them. They like to share their large home and work together to raise their babies. They teach their young how to find food and stay safe, just like our parents teach us important things.

The Rhythm of the Wild

Maned wolves live by the patterns of nature. They know when the seasons change and when it is time to have babies. They also move around at night, following the natural beat of their world.

Territorial Guardians

Defending the Den

The male maned wolf is like a brave knight who protects his home. He walks around his land, leaving smells to tell other animals that this is his family's place. He works hard to keep his mate and babies safe.

Patrols and Protection

When the sun goes down, the male keeps
watching over his family. He walks around
their home, always looking out for danger.
His eyes shine in the dark, and he is always
ready to protect his loved ones.

The Sentinel's Call

The male maned wolf howls to let other animals know he is there to keep his family
safe. His howl tells other animals to stay
away and tells his family that he is there for
them.

The Role of the Father

Provider of Nourishment

In the early morning, the father comes back from hunting with food
for his babies. His job is to make sure his family has what they need
to grow strong. He helps his babies learn about the land and feel
loved.

Playful and Protective

The father plays with his babies, teaching them about their home through fun games. He shows them love and teaches them to trust him.

Teacher of the Trails

The father shows his little ones the way around their home, making sure they know where to go. He helps them get ready for the day they will explore on their own.

Challenges in the Wild

Natural Threats

The maned wolf faces many problems. Their long legs help them in the fields, but they cannot always escape danger. Sometimes, there is not enough food, and humans take over their land. They must overcome many things to keep living in the wild.

Human Encroachment

Farms and cities are changing the quiet world of the maned wolves. Humans are taking more of their space. This is why we need to help save their homes and let them live in peace.

The Call for Coexistence

Maned wolves need our help to survive. We can work together to make sure they have a place in the wild. If we all respect and understand these animals, we can live together without problems.

Conservation of Maned Wolves

A Species at Risk

The maned wolf is in danger. People are taking over their homes, dividing them. These beautiful animals need our help to stay safe and keep the places where they live healthy.

Community Involvement

There are delightful stories about people working together to help maned wolves. People are fixing up their homes. They are also teaching each other to live peacefully with these wolves. These projects are important to keep maned wolves around for a long time.

Insights from Maned Wolf Dads

Lessons in Paternal Care

Male maned wolves are great dads. They show us that in the animal world, parents play different roles. By looking at how these dads care for their babies, we see that parents' help is vital. It is important for the babies to grow well.

The Bonds That Bind

Maned wolf dads and their babies have strong family ties. The dads help raise the pups, which makes them feel safe and loved. These close relationships are important for the pups as they grow.

Engaging Future Conservationists

Fascination with the Unique

We want to make kids excited about maned wolves and the special places they live in South America. By learning about these animals, kids can love nature more and want to take care of it.

Actions for the Wild

Kids can do a lot to help save animals like the maned wolf. By understanding why it is important to care for these animals and their homes, kids can protect them. It is also good for the environment.

Discover More About Maned Wolves

Interactive Learning Opportunities

We encourage kids to learn more about maned wolves by doing fun activities. They can do projects about where maned wolves live. They can join clubs that care about animals. Or they can help zoos that look after maned wolves.

Advocacy for Grassland Preservation

Kids can help save the big open fields where maned wolves live. By learning about these places, kids see the animals and plants that live there. They can see how everything works together and why it is important to keep it safe.

Conclusion: Protecting the Spirit of the Grasslands

Embracing Our Role as Stewards

Let us think about our job in taking care of the big fields where maned wolves live. These animals are not just cool to look at. They also help us understand their habitats. These habitats need our protection.

Acting for Conservation

Maned wolves need us to help them, no matter where we are. We need to do something to keep these special animals and their homes safe.

A Call to Preserve

Let us promise to look after the big fields and all the living things there. By helping save maned wolves and their homes, we are helping keep our planet full of life for the future.

Your Voice Matters

You can do a lot to help maned wolves, whether it is talking about them, helping with projects, or just loving nature. Together, we can change things, step by step.

Glossary

- **Canids:** This is a big family of animals that includes dogs, wolves, foxes, and other similar animals. Maned wolves are a part of this family.

- **Grasslands:** These are big, open fields where grasses, not trees, are the main plants. Maned wolves live in the grasslands of South America.

- **Mane:** This is the long, thick hair on the neck of some animals, like maned wolves and lions. For the maned wolf, it stands up when they want to look bigger or are scared.

- **Solitary:** When an animal likes to be alone most of the time, it's called solitary. Maned wolves usually live and do things on their own.

- **Mate:** This is a partner that an animal chooses to have babies with. Maned wolves usually have one mate for life.

- An animal is **territorial** if it has a certain area that it calls home. It will defend this area against others. Maned wolves are territorial, marking their space to let others know it's theirs.

- **Nocturnal animals** are active at night. They sleep during the day. Maned wolves do a lot of their hunting and moving around at night.

- **Human Encroachment** happens when people take over the places where wild animals live. This includes the grasslands for maned wolves. They do things like building farms and cities.

- **Endangered animals** are rare if there are not many left and they might die out. They are called endangered. Maned wolves are endangered because there are few left in the wild.

- **Stewardship:** This means taking care of something well. People can show stewardship for the environment.

Chapter 13: Bearded Dragons – Fathers of the Desert

Introduction to Bearded Dragons

Resilience in the Desert

Bearded dragons are amazing lizards that live in the desert.

Think about being in a spot where the sun is really hot all the time, making the ground very warm. That seems hard, doesn't it? But bearded dragons have special ways to handle it and do well living there.

Distinctive Traits

These dragons look special. They have spiky skin and a beard-like thing around their neck. These features help them hide from enemies and talk to other dragons without making a sound.

Surprising Paternal Behaviors

Bearded Dragons are not just tough on the outside; they are also great dads. They take care of their babies in the desert, which is a hard place to live.

Widespread Wanderers

Bearded Dragons live in many places, like dry deserts and rocky areas in Australia. They like different places like the beach and the bush too. Knowing where they live helps us understand how they can live in such hard places.

Understanding Bearded Dragon Societies

Solitude in the Sands

These dragons usually live alone, but they have a special way of acting when it is time to find a mate. They show us that even in a tough place like the desert, they can still have friends and family.

Comparing Desert Dwellers

We see this when we look at Bearded Dragons and other desert animals. These animals include geckos and tortoises. They all have different ways to live well in the desert. This helps us learn more about how desert animals live.

Territorial Guardians

Males: Masters of Their Domain

Male Bearded Dragons are very protective of their homes. They keep their area safe for their families and make sure other dragons know it is their space.

Marking Their Territory

They do things like nod their heads and puff out their beards to show other dragons that this is their place. This helps them keep their homes safe and find a mate.

Courtship Choreography: The Bearded Dragon Dance

The Rituals of Romance

Bearded Dragons do a special dance to find a mate. They move by nodding their heads and waving their arms. This dance tells other dragons they are ready to have babies.

Post-Mating Interactions

After they find a mate, Bearded Dragons do things to help their babies be healthy and safe. They make nests and keep an eye on their babies, which helps the babies grow up strong.

Fatherly Care: Guardians of the Hatchlings

Nurturing Instincts

Male Bearded Dragons are also good at taking care of their babies. They watch over the little ones and keep them safe, even though they usually like to be alone.

Lessons in Survival

The dad teaches the baby dragons how to live in the desert, like how to find food and stay safe. This helps the babies get ready to live on their own in the tough desert.

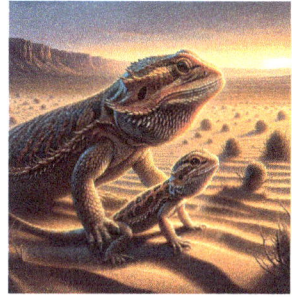

Surviving the Desert Wilderness

Adapting to Arid Realities

Bearded Dragons face many challenges in the desert, like very hot weather and not much food or water. But they have special ways to live well, even in such a hard place.

Predators of the Sands

There are dangers in the desert, like other animals that want to eat the dragons. Bearded Dragons must be smart and quick to stay safe from birds, snakes, and big lizards.

Tales of Triumph

These dragons have amazing stories of living through tough times in the desert. We can learn about their smart ways and how they manage to live in a place where it is hard to survive.

Conservation of Bearded Dragons

Protecting a Precious Species

Bearded Dragons are in danger. People are changing their habitats. The weather is getting hotter. Other human activities can hurt them. It is important to know how we can keep them safe.

Threats to Survival

People are building more cities and farms, which takes away the Bearded Dragons' homes. The weather is changing too, and that can make it harder for them to live in their natural places.

Conservation Initiatives

People are trying to help save Bearded Dragons. They make safe places for them, breed them in safe spots, and teach everyone why these dragons are special. We need to keep their homes healthy and safe for them to live.

Individual Contributions

Everyone can help save Bearded Dragons. You can help these cool dragons by things like using less energy. Also, by helping groups that protect wildlife. And by telling others how to keep animals safe.

Insights from Bearded Dragon Dads

Protective Guardians

Bearded Dragon dads are really good at taking care of their babies. They keep them safe just like human dads do with their kids.

Parallels with Human Paternal Care

Bearded Dragon dads care for their babies in ways that are a lot like how human dads care for their children. They both want to make sure their families are safe and happy.

Protection efforts for society

Bearded Dragon dads take great care of their kids. This shows us how important it is for all dads to be there for their families. When dads help with kid care, it's good for everyone.

Engaging Future Herpetologists

Dear young friends,

Do you love learning about snakes, lizards, frogs, and salamanders? You might be a herpetologist in the making. That's someone who studies these amazing animals!

Herpetologists help us take care of these creatures and their homes. They study how they live and why they are important to nature.

You can help these animals too! Try to find reptiles and amphibians where you live, visit museums, or be part of science projects. You can learn from people who know a lot about these animals and who work to protect them.

We all can help keep our world full of different kinds of life. Let's learn more about reptiles and amphibians together!

Good luck on your adventure into herpetology,

Shiva Kumar

Discover More About Bearded Dragons

Let's have fun learning about Bearded Dragons with these activities:

Habitat Modeling: Build a small desert home for Bearded Dragons. Use sand, rocks, and plants. This helps us understand how important it is to keep their real homes safe.

Citizen Science: Be part of projects that count Bearded Dragons. They show how many there are and where they live. Your help can give important information to scientists. They are trying to protect them.

Virtual Reality Applications: Use virtual reality to see the world of Bearded Dragons. You can visit their homes and watch them without leaving your house.

Conclusion: A Tribute to Bearded Dragon Dads

As we finish our story about Bearded Dragon dads, let's think about how amazing they are. They take really good care of their babies and show us that animal dads can be just as caring as human dads. As we keep learning about them, we might find out even more cool things about Bearded Dragon dads.

Glossary

- **Arid** describes places that are very dry and without much rain. It's like deserts where Bearded Dragons live.

- **Camouflage:** This is when an animal blends in with its surroundings to hide from predators or to sneak up on prey. Bearded Dragons can look like the sand and rocks they live around.

- **Territory:** This is an area that an animal, like a Bearded Dragon, claims as its own and will protect from others.

- **Habitat:** This is the natural home or environment where an animal lives. Bearded Dragons' habitats are the hot, dry deserts of Australia.

- **Carnivore:** This means 'meat eater'. Baby Bearded Dragons are mostly carnivores, eating things like insects.

- **Omnivore:** This is an animal that eats both plants and meat. Adult Bearded Dragons are omnivores.

- **Herpetology:** This is the study of reptiles and amphibians. Herpetologists learn all about creatures like Bearded Dragons.

- **Ectothermic** is a scientific word. It describes animals that need warmth from their environment to heat their bodies. Bearded Dragons get warm by basking in the sun.

- **Predator:** These are animals that hunt and eat other animals. Bearded Dragons can eat insects, but they have to watch out for predators. Predators include birds and snakes.

- **Conservation** is the work of taking care of our natural world. It includes animals and plants. The goal is to make sure they are around for a long time.

- **Brumation:** This is like hibernation for cold-blooded animals. Bearded Dragons may brumate, or take a long rest, during the colder months when food is scarce.

- **Viviparous** animals give birth to live young. They do not lay eggs. Bearded Dragons are not viviparous; they lay eggs.

Chapter 14: Grevy's Zebras – Guardians of the Savannah

Introduction to Grevy's Zebras

Welcome to the Home of Grevy's Zebras

M eet Grevy's zebras. They are special horses with stripes and live in the grasslands of East Africa.

They got their name from Jules Grevy, a leader from France who got one as a special present. These zebras are amazing to see. They have bold stripes in black and white and move in a smooth and elegant way. They walk around the wide places under the bright sun.

Mystery of Zebra Dads

There is a lot we know about how Grevy's zebras live and behave, but one secret remains: their life as dads. Few people talk about the key roles zebra fathers play. They play them with their families and the savannah. We are about to go on an exciting journey. We will uncover how these striped heroes care for their loved ones and protect their home.

Savannah Protectors

Grevy's zebras do amazing things for their family and the savannah, their home. They teach us about caring for others and the importance of family. By learning about their lives, we can discover more about the animals and the land of the African plains. This shows us the beauty and complexity of nature.

Territory Matters

Establishing Dominance

Male Grevy's zebras like to show who is boss by claiming areas as their own. They show their strength and sometimes fight with other males to keep control of the best spots. These zebras use smells and even fights to show they are in charge. This helps them figure out who is the leader in their groups.

A Haven for Mating

The areas these zebras' control is not just for showing who is strongest; they also matter when it is time to find a mate. Female zebras like males with their own territory. It means they have lots of food and can keep them safe. So, for male zebras, having a good spot is key to finding a mate and having baby zebras.

Social Structure and Stability

The places where zebras live are the foundation of how they have a good relationship with each other. Inside each area, the strongest male looks after a group of females. This helps keep everyone organized and safe. These male zebras make sure everyone knows where they belong. This helps their groups stay together and their baby zebras grow up safely.

Zebra Rivalries

Battling for Dominance: Intense Competition

Male Grevy's zebras often compete for the best territories and chances to find a mate. They can get into fights where they show off, make loud sounds, and sometimes even battle. They check each other out to see who is the toughest and who deserves to be the leader.

Displaying Superiority

To prove they are the best, male Grevy's zebras do many things. They stand tall, make noise, and run fast to scare off other males. These actions tell everyone that they are strong and make good leaders and partners.

Strategic Maneuvers

When fighting for their territories, male Grevy's zebras must think fast and be clever. They might try to sneak around other males or surprise them to win the fight. Being smart and quick helps, then beat their rivals and become the top zebra.

The Zebras' Watchful Eye

Sentinel Duty: Vigilant Guardians

Male Grevy's zebras are always on the look-out for danger. They use their sharp eyes and ears to spot predators from far away. This helps them tell the other zebras when to be careful and how to stay safe.

Defending the Herd: Swift Response

If predators come close, male Grevy's zebras are quick to protect their herd. They get everyone together to fight off danger. They are brave and work hard to keep the predators away from the little ones.

Maintaining Cohesion

Male zebras are important for keeping everyone in the group working together. They watch out for danger and help everyone feel safe. This makes the group strong and helps all the zebras live well together.

The Role of a Grevy's Zebra Dad

Beyond Territory Defense: Nurturing Fathers

Grevy's zebra dads do more than just guard their land; they also take great care of their foals (young zebras). These dads show their love by spending lots of time helping their little ones grow up strong and smart. They teach them how to find food, have a good relationship with others, and stay safe from predators.

Firsthand Parenting

Zebra dads engage in raising their foals. They are patient. They pay close attention to what their foals need. They show them how to live and survive on the savannah.

Collaborative Parenting: Partnering with Mothers

Dad zebras collaborate with mom zebras to take care of their foals. Together, they are a super team. They make sure their foals have all they need, like food and safety, as they grow up.

Shared Responsibilities

In a zebra family, both mom and dad share the job of looking after the foals. They each use their own unique skills to help raise their young ones. This teamwork helps the baby zebras become strong and healthy.

A Haven for Young

Importance of a Secure Territory: Ensuring Safety and Growth

For baby zebras to be safe and grow up well, they need a good place to live. Their home gives them protection and all the things they need, like food and water. Dad zebras keep watch to keep their families safe. Their home is a perfect place for little zebras to learn and play.

Sheltering the Vulnerable

The zebra's home is like a safe playground where the foals can have fun without worrying about danger. It is a place where they feel safe and can grow up to be brave and strong.

Social Bonds within the Family Unit: Strong Family Ties

Zebras have a close family where everyone takes care of each other. Dad zebras bond with their foals. This makes the family tight-knit and caring.

Learning from Elders

Young zebras learn a lot from their parents and other older zebras. They watch and copy them to learn how to live and survive. They pass down important lessons from one generation to the next.

Lessons from Grevy's Zebras: Teamwork and Protective Strategies

Collaborative Defense

Zebras teach us how working together can help everyone stay safe. They stick together to keep their land, watch out for danger, and take care of their foals. This shows us that teaming up is a wonderful way to face problems.

Adaptive Resilience

Zebras are great at dealing with changes and tough situations. They can manage different challenges, like finding food or escaping predators. This shows us that being flexible and strong can help us get through tough times.

Ecological Importance

Keystone Species

Grevy's zebras are important to their environment. They eat grass and plants, which helps keep the land healthy and stops too much of one plant from growing. This is good for other plants and animals too. When zebras are around, they also become food for animals like lions. This is part of how nature stays in balance.

Indicator Species

These zebras can also tell us if their home is healthy. We see few zebras or they are not doing well. This might mean bigger problems, like too little food, too much heat, or people changing the land.

Human Applications

Teamwork and Collaboration

We can learn from zebras about how to work well with others. They show us that when we work as a team and share the work, we can do wonderful things. This can help us in school, at work, or with our families.

Adaptive Thinking

Zebras are also good at dealing with changes and finding new ways to solve problems. This teaches us to think differently and be ready to change when we need to. This can help us when things get tough.

Conclusion

Grevy's zebras teach us about being together as a team, staying strong, and taking care of the world around us. By learning about these amazing animals, we understand more about nature. We also learn how we should care for it.

Learn more about Grevy's zebras and help protect them. This will teach the next generation to care about animals and the world. Together, we can make sure that zebras and other animals will always have a wonderful place to live.

Glossary

- **Grevy's Zebra:** A type of zebra with large ears and narrow stripes, found in Eastern Africa. They are the largest type of zebra.

- **Savannah:** A grassy plain in tropical and subtropical regions with few trees. It's the natural habitat of the Grevy's zebra.

- **Territory:** An area that an animal, like a male Grevy's zebra, claims as its own and defends from others.

- **Dominance:** When one zebra acts as the leader of a group and makes decisions, often by showing its strength.

- **Mating:** The process by which animals pair up to have babies. For zebras, this usually happens within the territory of the male.

- **Social Structure:** The way a group of animals, like a herd of zebras, is organized. This includes who leads the group and how others follow.

- **Predator:** An animal that hunts and eats other animals. Lions and hyenas are predators of zebras.

- **Foal:** A baby zebra.

- **Conservation:** The act of protecting and preserving natural resources and the environment. This includes protecting their habitat and stopping poaching.

- A **keystone species** has a big impact on its environment. Without it, the ecosystem would change a lot. Grevy's zebras are considered a keystone species because they help maintain the savannah.

- **Indicator Species:** Animals that can give scientists a sign of the health of the ecosystem. If the zebras are doing well, it usually means the environment is healthy too.

- **Adaptations** are changes in an animal's behavior or body. They help it survive better in its environment. Grevy's zebras have adapted to living in hot, dry places with little water.

Part III

African Wild Dogs, Giant Otters, Praire Voles, Golden Lion Tamarins, Hornbills, Silky Anteaters, and Harp Seals.

Chapter 15: African Wild Dogs: Guardians of the Pack

Introduction to African Wild Dogs

Meet the Painted Wolves

Picture a dog that is special, with fur that's all sorts of colors, like it was painted by the world itself.

This dog is called the African Wild Dog. Some people call it the painted wolf. They do so because it looks so different and colorful. These wild dogs are super good at working together in a team. They are some of the top hunters in Africa, and they move together across the big, open grasslands. Watching them teaches us how important it is to

work with others. When they team up, they can take on tough tasks that would be too hard for just one dog.

Where They Live

African Wild Dogs like to wander around the plains and forests of sub-Saharan Africa. They used to be found in many places, but now it is harder for them to find homes because people are changing the land. This makes it hard for them to find food and safe places to live, so we need to help protect their homes.

Exploring the Wild Home of African Wild Dogs

Home Sweet Home: Where They Roam

African Wild Dogs have bright, colorful coats. They live all over Africa. Picture huge savannas. The grass waves in the wind. See thick forests with tall trees. And even hot deserts. These animals do not stay in one place; they have homes from Botswana to Zimbabwe and South Africa. They are happy anywhere there is enough space to move around and hunt.

Adaptable Adventurers

These painted wolves can live anywhere. They might stay in open grasslands or hide in thick woods. Even places changed by people, like farms, can be where they live. This ability to adapt helps them find food and take care of their families, no matter where they are.

Leaders of the Land: Nature's Balance Keepers

Imagine if one animal ate all the grass and left none for others. That would not be good. African Wild Dogs help make sure that does not happen. They hunt as a team and keep the numbers of other animals exactly right. This helps the plants and the whole environment stay healthy. African Wild Dogs are like nature's superheroes, keeping everything in balance.

The Power of Teamwork: Life in an African Wild Dog Pack

The Wild Dog Family: Leaders of the Pack

Think of a big family where everyone has a role. That is how African Wild Dog packs work. The mom and dad, called the alpha pair, are in charge. They decide everything from where to hunt to where to sleep. They lead their wild dog family wisely and strongly.

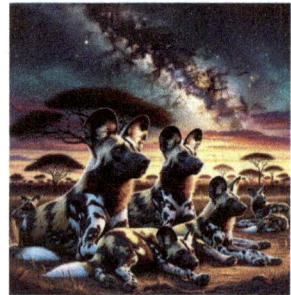

Team Members

In this family, everyone helps. Aunts, uncles, and even neighbors help with the pups. They babysit and teach the pups about the wild while the parents hunt. This teamwork keeps the family strong, fed, and safe.

Future Stars

The pups are the youngest and have a lot to learn. They are like students, learning how to hunt and survive from the adults. The pack is like a school, with every adult ready to teach and every pup eager to learn.

The Hunt

Teamwork Makes the Dream Work

When it is time to eat, African Wild Dogs show off their teamwork. They get excited together before they go hunting. Then they use their sharp senses to find food.

Strategy and Speed

They chase, outsmart, and tire out their prey. They are like a sports team that works together to win. Their teamwork lets them catch bigger animals, showing they are stronger together.

Sharing is Caring: A Family Meal

After hunting, the older dogs do not forget about the pups at home. They eat and then bring back food for the pups and the mom. They share the food, teaching the pups about caring for the whole family.

Unity and Empathy

In the world of African Wild Dogs, teamwork and caring for each other are important every day. Their lives are about living well together, not just alone. These wild dogs teach us about unity and looking out for each other, making sure no one is left behind.

Fatherhood in African Wild Dogs: The Role of Dad

The Dad's Contribution

In African Wild Dog families, dads are much more than pack members; they are key to their family's success. They do important jobs. They hunt for food and teach their pups key skills. Their job is to protect their family from danger and help their pups learn how to be part of the group.

Guidance and Safeguarding

These dads are always watching for danger and are also the pack's teachers. They play with their pups to teach them key skills. These include hunting and learning pack behavior. This hands-on parenting ensures the pups will grow up ready for anything.

Quality Time Together

Dads have a deep bond with their pups. They show love by grooming them, sharing food by bringing it back up, and playing. This care strengthens the family bond and is important for the pups' growth and health.

Fatherhood in African Wild Dogs shows how vital active parenting is. It is vital for the pack's survival and well-being. It is about the whole family working together and caring for each other.

United for Survival: Saving the African Wild Dogs

Understanding Through Research

Scientists study African Wild Dogs to learn what they need to survive. They use things like radio collars and DNA tests to track their health and numbers. This helps conservationists know how to help them.

Partnership with People

Saving African Wild Dogs is also about work-ing with the people who live near them. Conservation is about helping the animals and the people. We can protect the dogs. We can improve lives by educating people. And we can start programs to help them live with the dogs.

Teaching for Conservation

Spreading Knowledge

Teaching people about African Wild Dogs is key to getting support for conservation. Groups use social media and other tools. They share info about these dogs and why they are important. These stories help people understand why we need to protect all parts of nature.

Inspiring Young Protectors

It is important to tutor young people about conservation. Conservationists work with schools to create lessons and activities about African Wild Dogs. This helps students learn about nature and how to protect it.

Planning for African Wild Dogs

Facing Future Problems

African Wild Dogs have many challenges ahead. They need big con-servation efforts. They also need the latest ideas and help from communities to survive. Yet, there are also chances to use new sci-ence and people's help to make things better for these dogs.

A Ray of Hope

There are good signs for African Wild Dogs. Many groups are working to protect them and their homes. By working together, we can face the challenges and help these dogs live safely in the wild.

Honoring the Fathers of the Wild: A Tribute to African Wild Dog Dads

Let us celebrate the amazing dads in African Wild Dog packs. They work hard to feed their families and teach their pups. Their mix of bravery, knowledge, and kindness is special and shows how impor-tant they are to the pack.

A United Call to Action

African Wild Dog dads are strong and committed to their families. They show us we must protect these great animals and their homes. It is a call for everyone to help save this species. We can support conservation projects. We can get involved in our communities. Or we can just tell others about these dogs and the work to save them. Every little bit helps in the battle to keep these canine families safe and healthy in Africa.

Glossary

- The **African Wild Dog** (Painted Wolf) is a unique type of wild canine. It is known for its colorful, patchy coat, which looks like a painting. These dogs are excellent team hunters and live in packs across Africa.

- **Savannahs** are large, open grasslands. They are found in Africa. Many animals, including the African Wild Dog, live there. These areas have few trees and are home to diverse wildlife.

- **Pack:** A group of African Wild Dogs that live, hunt, and do everything together. The pack is like a big family with strong bonds between its members.

- **Alpha Pair:** The leading male and female in a pack of African Wild Dogs. They make important decisions for the pack, such as when and where to hunt.

- **Territory** is the specific area that a pack of African Wild Dogs calls home. They defend it against other packs or predators.

- **Predator:** Animals that hunt other animals for food. African Wild Dogs are predators, but they also have to be careful of larger predators like lions.

- **Pup:** A baby African Wild Dog. Pups depend on the entire pack for protection, food, and learning how to survive in the wild.

- **Habitat:** The natural environment where a species lives. African Wild Dogs live in savannahs and woodlands. They also live on the edges of deserts.

- **Sub-Saharan Africa:** The part of Africa located south of the Sahara Desert. This region is home to many unique animals, including the African Wild Dog.

- **Endangered:** A term used to describe species at risk of extinction. African Wild Dogs are endangered. This is because they have lost habitat, have had disease, and have had conflict with humans.

- **Ecosystem Balance:** The natural harmony among different species and their environment. African Wild Dogs play a crucial role. They do this by controlling prey numbers.

Chapter 16: River Giants: The Giant Otter Families of South America

Introduction to Giant Otters

Majestic Aquatic Mammals

G iant otters are huge river animals from South America. They are the biggest otters and are good at swimming and catching food. They are smart and move around their water homes with grace and strength.

A Family Affair

Giant otter families have wonderful dads who help teach and look after their babies. These dads are important in their families. They show their little ones how to find food and swim well. The families stick together and help each other out.

The Habitat of the Giant Otter

Watery Realm Explored

Giant otters live in the beautiful, watery lands of South America. They have homes in rivers, lakes, and wetlands that are full of life. These places have lots of fish, which the otters eat. They need these waterways to live, to find food, and to have space for their families. These areas are full of different plants and animals, and the otters are a big part of this lively world.

Defending the Domain

Giant otters really care about where they live. They want to make sure their families have the best places to find food and be safe. They keep other animals out of their space to make sure they have what they need. By doing this, they keep everything balanced in their water home.

Parenthood in the Otter World

Duties of an Otter Father

Giant otter dads are like heroes. They do not just keep their families safe; they are also teachers and protectors. They teach their babies to swim, find food, and play. These dads watch over their families all the time to keep them safe from danger. They make sure their babies grow up to be strong and able otters.

Learning as a Family

Growing up as a giant otter means learning a lot, and everyone in the family helps. Baby otters watch and copy what their parents and siblings do. They learn together and help each other. They hunt, play, and clean each other as a team. This shows how important family and working together are for these otters.

The Father's Teaching: Skills for Survival

Hunting Lessons

Giant otter dads are great at catching food, and they teach this to their babies. They show them how to find and grab fish in the water. This is important for the babies to learn so they can take care of themselves. Watching a dad otter teach fishing is like seeing a special family tradition.

Guardian of the Den

The dad otter does more than teach; he also keeps his family safe. He makes sure nothing dangerous comes near the home where the babies can grow and learn safely. This makes their home a cozy and happy place.

Emotional Support

Giant otter dads give love and comfort too. They cuddle and play with their babies, which helps them feel happy and safe. This love helps the babies learn how to be good friends and family members when they grow up.

Leading the Hunt

When it is time to find food, the dad otter is a great leader. He helps the family work together to catch fish. They all move together in the water to get their meal. This is not just about eating; it is also about learning to work as a team and help each other.

Challenges of Life in the River

Navigating Dangers

Living in the river can be tough for giant otter families. They must watch out for predators. They also deal with problems caused by people, like losing their homes and dirty water. People cut down trees and pollute. This can make it hard for otters to find food and safe places to live. Discussing these problems is important. It helps us know we need to care for these special animals and their homes.

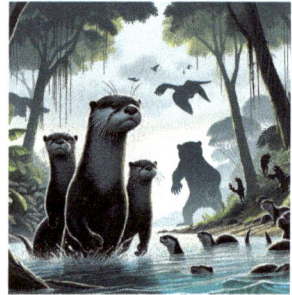

Adaptive Masters

Giant otters are good at dealing with problems. They stick together as families and help each other out, which helps them stay alive. They talk to each other in special ways to make plans and deal with changes in their homes. They can also change what they eat and how they hunt if they need to. This shows how amazing giant otters are at living in the river, even when it is hard.

The Social Life of Giant Otters

Voices of the River

The rivers where giant otters live are full of their special sounds. They make different noises to talk to each other, warn about danger, and make plans for hunting. Their sounds help them stay close as a family and help each other out in the big, watery world they live in.

The Joy of Play

Playing is important for giant otters. It is how the little otters learn to hunt, fight, and be with others, all while having fun with their family. Even the grown-ups play to stay close and happy together. Watching otters play is wonderful as they slide, splash, and chase each other. Playing helps them learn and keep their family strong.

Conservation of the Giant Otter

Under Threat

Giant otters, the beautiful animals of South America's rivers, are in danger. They face many problems. They include losing their homes, dirty water, and sometimes people hunting them. Changes in the weather also hurt the places where they live and can make it hard to find food. We need to understand these problems. Doing so will help protect giant otters and all the other living things in their homes.

Conservation Efforts

People are working hard to help giant otters and their homes. They do things like care for otter habitats. They also stop hunting. And they teach people how to help. There are safe areas for otters. Scientists are learning more about otters to help protect them. Telling people about how otters need help can make more people care and want to help, too.

Inspiring Young Conservationists

Future Protectors

You can help protect animals like giant otters. You can learn about how to take care of animals and tell your friends and family. Helping to clean up rivers and lakes. Or helping animal groups. Both can make a significant difference. Every little thing you do helps, and young people like you can help keep our world full of life.

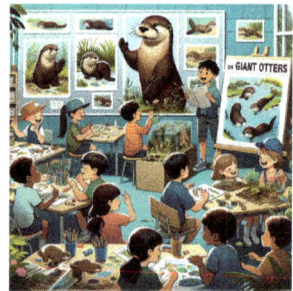

Otter Inspired Activities

To learn more about giant otters and to help them, try these fun things:

Adopt an Otter: Help protect otters by adopting one. You will learn a lot about them!

Create an Otter Habitat Model: Make a model of where otters live using things you can recycle. It helps you understand why it is important to keep their homes safe.

Visit a Zoo or Aquarium: See how otters live and learn about how to protect them by visiting them at a zoo or aquarium.

Conservation Art Project: Make art about otters and where they live. Art can help others learn about how to protect otters.

Learn and Share: Find out more about giant otters and share what you learn with your school or community. Talking about otters is an effective way to help them.

Lesser-Known Facts About Giant Otters

Remarkable Vocalists

Giant otters are good at making different sounds—over twenty of them! These sounds help them talk to their families and work together. Each noise they make has a special meaning and helps them live together in the river.

Impressive Builders

Giant otters are not only good swimmers; they are also great at building homes. They make dens by the river with different rooms and doors. These homes keep them safe and cozy.

Social Learners

Giant otters learn a lot from their families. The younger ones watch and do what the older ones do. This helps them learn important things like how to hunt and stay safe. Learning from each other also keeps them close and helps them all do well together.

A Keen Sense of Territory

Giant otter families are very protective of their homes along the river. They keep a close watch over their own space, which can be a long stretch of the riverbank. This way, they make sure they have all the food and safe places to rest that they need. This shows how smart they are about living to-gether. It is why having their own territory is vital for staying alive.

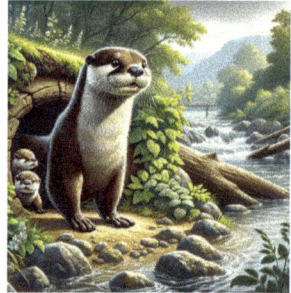

Unique to South America

Giant otters are special animals that only live in the fresh waters of South America. They are a big part of what makes the continent's nature so rich and interesting. When we take care of giant otters, we also take care of the special places where they live. This is important for the entire world, not South America alone.

Conclusion: A Tribute to Giant Otter Dads

Giant Otter dads are amazing. They live in the beautiful rivers of South America and take safe care of their families. They teach and protect their little ones and help keep everything in nature balanced.

We want to say a big thank you to the Giant Otter dads. They show us how important each creature is to the world. We need to make sure these otters and their homes stay safe. This is important for the health of our planet's rivers and all the animals and plants that live there.

Glossary

- **Giant Otters:** Big river animals from South America that are the largest kind of otters. They are excellent swimmers and hunters in the water.

- **Aquatic mammals** live in water and breathe air. They include whales, dolphins, and otters. They have special adaptations to live in water but come up to breathe.

- **Habitat:** The natural home of an animal or plant. Giant otters live in rivers, lakes, and wetlands. They find food and live there with their families.

- **Wetlands:** Land areas that are often or always soaked with water. They are important for lots of plants and animals because they provide food and a place to live.

- **Social Learners:** Animals that learn from watching and copying others in their group. Giant otters learn important skills by watching their families.

- **Territory:** An area that an animal or a group of animals uses and defends as their own. Giant otter families have their own territories along rivers.

- **Adaptation** is a unique feature or behavior. It helps an animal survive in its environment. Giant otters have adaptations. They have strong swimming skills and can communicate with sounds.

- **Vocalizations:** The sounds animals make to communicate with each other. Giant otters use more than twenty different sounds to talk to their family members.

Chapter 17: Prairie Voles – Guardians of Family Bonds

Introduction to Prairie Voles

Prairie voles are cute, furry animals. Prairies are the big open lands in North America where they live. Running around and digging holes in the ground is what they do. They play a key role in keeping nature balanced where they live. They also love to stick together in families, showing us how special friendships can be even in the animal world.

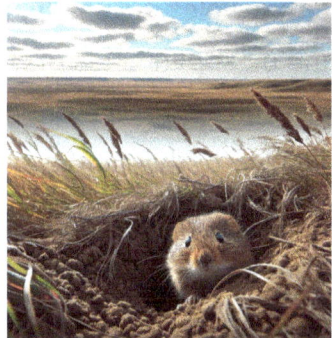

Charm of the Prairies

Prairies are sunny places with lots of grass
and flowers, and prairie voles call this place
home. You can find them making paths
and tunnels here, adding life to this peaceful place. They show us how many different kinds of living things there are in the
prairies.

Fascinating Behavior

Prairie voles may be small, but they do many amazing things. They
make tunnels under the ground and have special ways of living
together. They choose one partner to stay with and take really good
care of their babies. Watching them helps us learn about how families work in the wild.

Geographical Spread

Prairie voles are small animals that live in
the big, open fields of North America. You
can find them from the bottom of Canada all
the way to the middle of the United States.
They are good at living in various places.
Even when it's tough because their homes
are disappearing. Prairie voles keep living.
They are strong. We should care for the fields and lands they need
to survive.

Prairie Vole Social Structure

Formation of Pair Bonds

Prairie voles are special because they stick with just one partner. These strong connections are important for how they live together. They do a little dance and send special smells to show they like each other. Then, they stay together. This helps them have babies and stay healthy.

Family Units

Prairie voles have families with a mom, a dad, and their babies. Both the mom and the dad help take care of the little ones. They build nests, clean each other, and all work together. This helps the baby voles grow up strong and keeps the prairie vole families close.

Nest Building and Home Life

Nest Construction

Dad prairie voles work hard to make nests for their families. They use grass and leaves to make a cozy home for their babies. This shows how much they care about keeping their family safe and warm.

Family Dynamics

Inside their nests, prairie voles have a happy family life. The parents take care of the babies by keeping them warm and clean. They play and cuddle together, which helps the little voles learn and feel loved.

Courtship and Mating Rituals

Courtship Displays

Dad prairie voles try to impress the mom voles with special dances and sounds. They do this to show they would be a good partner. This helps them find someone to make a family with.

Pair Bond Formation

When prairie voles like each other, they spend a lot of time together, grooming and exploring. This helps them become a pair that will take care of each other and their babies. They work as a team to make sure their family is happy.

Parental Responsibilities

Nest Maintenance

Dad prairie voles keep the nest in good shape. They fix it up and make it nice for their family. This helps everyone stay safe and comfortable.

Grooming and Protection

Dad voles also clean their family's fur and watch out for danger. This helps keep everyone in the family healthy and safe.

Nurturing the Young

Birth and Care

When baby prairie voles are born, both the mom and dad help take care of them. The dad helps clean and warm the babies, showing right away how much they are loved.

Feeding and Comfort

Dad voles help feed the babies and keep them snug and warm. This helps the little voles grow up healthy and strong.

Communication and Coordination

Vocalizations

Prairie voles make different sounds to talk to each other in their families. The dad voles make calls and chirps to tell about food, danger, and to chat with each other. These sounds help them stay close as a family and keep their bond strong.

Coordination in Parenting

Mom and dad prairie voles work together very well to take care of their babies. They use sounds and body language to talk to each other so they can do a good job of looking after their little ones. They share the work of building the nest, finding food, and cleaning their babies. This teamwork is important for their babies to grow up healthy.

Challenges in Prairie Life

Predation Risks

Prairie voles must watch out for animals that might want to eat them, like hawks, snakes, and foxes. They have smart ways to stay safe, like hiding underground and in thick grass.

Environmental Pressures

Farming and cities are growing. They are making the places where prairie voles live smaller. This makes it hard for them to find places to live and food to eat. The weather is also changing a lot, which can make life tough for them. We need to take care of their homes to help them stay safe.

Conservation Efforts

Habitat Preservation

People who want to help prairie voles are trying to keep their homes safe. They find important places where the voles live and make sure they are protected. They also try to fix places that are not good for voles anymore so they can live there again.

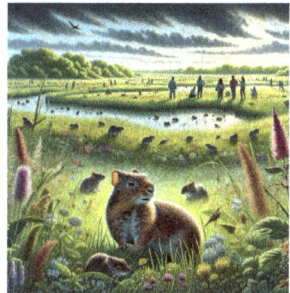

Community Involvement

It is important for people who live near prairies to help take care of them. They know a lot about the land and can help a lot. Teaching people about prairie voles is key. It helps everyone work together to keep the prairies safe.

Inspiring Future Stewards

Educational Outreach

You can help prairie voles by teaching others about them. Share what you know at school or events. It will help people understand why we need to protect prairies and the animals that live there.

Youth Engagement

Work with other kids who care about nature to help prairie voles. You can plant new grass, watch animals to learn about them, and tell people why we should take care of the land. By standing up for prairies, you can help save them for animals and people in the future.

Conclusion: Prairie Vole Champions

Prairie voles are amazing at taking care of their families and living in the prairie. They show us how every little animal is important for keeping nature healthy.

Let us remember how important it is to help prairie voles and keep the prairie full of life.

If we all work together, we can ensure that prairies are a good home for voles. They are home to many other plants and animals too. Let us promise to be friends of the prairie and take care of it for a long, long time.

Glossary

- **Prairie:** A large open area of grassland where there are few trees. Prairies are often found in North America, and many animals, like prairie voles, live there.

- **Voles:** Small, mouse-like rodents that have short tails, small ears, and a chunky body. Prairie voles are a type of vole that lives in the prairies.

- **Tunnels** are underground passageways. Animals, such as prairie voles, dig burrows. They use them to travel, live, and hide from predators.

- **Pair Bond:** A special connection between two animals who choose to stay together. Prairie voles form pair bonds and have a partner they live with and raise babies with.

- **Nest:** A cozy and safe place where animals, such as prairie voles, sleep, and take care of their young ones. It is often made of grass, leaves, or other soft materials.

- An **ecosystem** is a community of living things, like plants and animals. They work together with their environment in a certain area. Prairies are a type of ecosystem.

- **Predator:** An animal that hunts other animals for food. For prairie voles, predators can include hawks, snakes, and foxes.

- **Habitat:** The natural environment where a plant or animal lives. For prairie voles, their habitat includes grasslands and underground burrows.

- **Conservation** is the protection of nature and wildlife. It includes animals like prairie voles and their habitats. The goal is to make sure they are not harmed or destroyed.

- **Grooming:** When animals clean themselves or each other. Prairie vole parents groom their babies to keep them clean and healthy.

- **Vocalizations:** The sounds animals make to communicate. Prairie voles make chirps and squeaks to talk to their family and warn them of danger.

- **Foraging:** The act of searching for food. Prairie voles forage for seeds, plants, and insects to eat.

Chapter 18: Golden Lion Tamarins – Fatherhood in the Treetops

Introduction to Golden Lion Tamarins

Golden Lion Tamarins are cute, little monkeys with bright orange fur.

They have big smiles that make everyone happy. They sort of look like tiny lions because of the orange hair around their heads. These monkeys live in large, green forests where they love to play and jump around. They are special animals to see. They can make anyone love them just by being themselves.

Paternal Excellence

Golden Lion Tamarins are amazing because the dads are great at taking care of their babies. They help a lot with the babies and do things that most monkey dads do not do. We will learn about how these monkey families live together high in trees. We will also learn how the dads help their babies survive.

Geographical Spread

You can find Golden Lion Tamarins in the forests near the coast of Brazil. Their homes are in danger because the forests are being cut down. But these monkeys are strong and make people want to protect the forests where they live.

Life in the Treetops

Arboreal Home

Golden Lion Tamarins are exceptionally good at climbing and living in the trees. They have strong hands and feet that help them move through the tree branches. The trees are where they find food and stay safe from animals that might hurt them.

Family Dynamics

In Golden Lion Tamarin families, everyone stays close together. They live with their mom, dad, brothers, sisters, and sometimes other family members. The dad is busy with the babies. He cleans them, carries them, and feeds them. This helps the whole family stay strong and safe in the trees.

Tamarin Twins

Twin Phenomenon

These monkeys often have twins, which is not common in the animal world. Having two babies at once means the parents must work harder. But twins are good for the monkey family. They keep their numbers up, even when life gets tough in the forest.

Parental Roles

Both monkey parents are important for taking care of the babies. The dad has a special job of carrying the twins around. This helps the babies get the love and safety they need, and it lets the mom look for food without worrying.

Fatherly Duties

Beyond Carrying

The dad does more than just carry the babies. He keeps them warm and safe. This
helps the babies grow up strong in the trees.
Dad's work is important for the family.

Contributions to Well-being

The dad helps the babies stay away from dangers and grow up
healthy. His hard work is important for the family to do well in their
home in the trees.

Teaching and Play

Educational Play

Golden Lion Tamarin dads also play with
their babies. They use playtime to teach
them important things. They learn how to
find food, avoid danger, and get along with
others. Playing is fun and helps babies learn.

Teamwork in Parenting

The mom and dad monkey work together to take care of their babies. They each do different things to make sure their babies are

happy and healthy. Working as a team is a big part of being a Golden Lion Tamarin parent and keeps the family strong.

Challenges in the Jungle

Facing Threats

Golden Lion Tamarins face tough challenges in their jungle homes. They must watch out for predators like big birds and snakes that can harm the little monkeys. Also, people are cutting down the forests in Brazil where they live. This makes it even harder for them to survive. This is a big problem because there may be fewer monkeys if their homes keep disappearing.

Conservation in Action

Even though things look hard for the Golden Lion Tamarins, there are people working to help them. Projects are being done to grow more trees where forests were cut down. This gives the monkeys more places to live. People are also trying to keep the forests safe from being destroyed. We can really help the Golden Lion Tamarins. We can do this by working with people who live there, scientists, and groups that want to save animals.

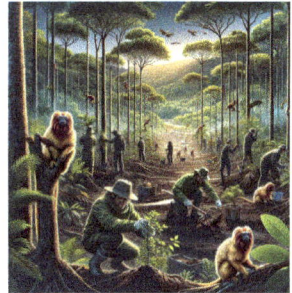

The Future of Golden Lion Tamarins

Conservation Successes

There is good news! Demanding work saved their homes and kept them safe. Now, there are more Golden Lion Tamarins in some places. This shows that when we really try, we can help save animals that are in danger. We see that these monkeys can do well again if we take loving care of their homes.

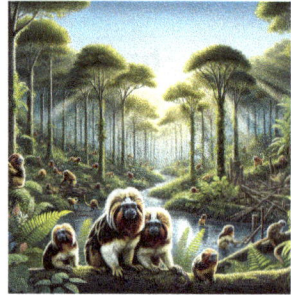

Human Impact and Responsibility

But we still have more work to do. Our actions can make life hard for the Golden Lion Tamarins. We need to keep helping them by taking care of the forests and not letting people take them from their homes. It is up to all of us to make sure we do things that are good for the monkeys and the places where they live.

Inspiring Young Conservationists

From Learning to Action

Learn all about these special monkeys and share with friends and family why we need to protect them. When we know more, we can help better.

Conservation Steps

You can do a lot to help! You can join a group that cleans up parks or share cool monkey facts online. Every little bit helps the monkeys.

Discover More About Golden Lion Tamarins

Here are some fun ways to get involved and help save the Golden Lion Tamarins:

Engagement Activities

Artistic Inspiration: Artistic Inspiration: Draw or make something. It should show the coolness of the Golden Lion Tamarins.

Habitat Exploration: Find out where these monkeys live and what they do every day.

Joining Conservation Efforts

Volunteer Opportunities: See if you can help with groups. They work to save the Golden Lion Tamarins.

Fundraising Initiatives: You could help raise money for the monkeys. You could make crafts to sell or set up an online fundraiser.

Advocacy and Education: Tell others about why we should save these monkeys and what they can do to help.

Conclusion: A Tribute to Golden Lion Tamarin Dads

Let us give a big cheer for the daddy monkeys! They are impressive at taking care of their families. By helping to save these monkeys, we make sure they can be happy and safe in the jungle for a long time.

Glossary

- **Golden Lion Tamarin:** This is a small monkey that shines bright orange, like a little lion. They live in Brazil's rainforests.

- **Arboreal:** This fancy word means they love to live up in trees! Golden Lion Tamarins spend most of their time swinging and jumping from branch to branch.

- **Father Tamarins:** Daddy tamarins are super dads! They take great care of their babies. This is cool compared to other monkey families.

- **Geographical Spread:** This just means where in the world you can find these monkeys. For Golden Lion Tamarins, they only live in the forests near Brazil's beaches.

- **Twin Phenomenon:** These monkeys often have twins, which is rare for monkeys. This means mom tamarins usually have two babies at a time, not just one.

- **Parental Roles:** This is all about the jobs mom and dad monkeys have in taking care of their kids. Golden Lion Tamarin dads and moms both work hard to look after their babies.

- **Conservation:** This is when people work to keep animals and their homes safe. For these monkeys, it means planting new trees. They must also ensure their forests are protected.

- **Predators:** These are animals that might want to eat the tamarins, like big birds or snakes. The tamarins have to be careful to stay safe.

- An **ecosystem** is a group of living things, like plants and animals. They live together and help each other. Golden Lion Tamarins are an important part of the rainforest family in Brazil.

- **Endangered:** This means there aren't many Golden Lion Tamarins left, and we have to work hard to make sure they don't disappear forever.

- **Reforestation** is when people plant new trees. They do this in places where forests were cut down. This is important. It gives Golden Lion Tamarins their homes back.

- **Habitat Exploration:** This is when we learn all about where animals live. By exploring where Golden Lion Tamarins live, we can find out how to help them better.

Chapter 19: Hornbills – Guardians of the Nest

Introduction to Hornbills

Hornbills are big, colorful birds that live in the jungle.

They have large beaks and make loud sounds. They are very caring and take care of their families well. Hornbill dads are great at keeping their nests safe. They live there with their families.

The Habitat of Hornbills

You can find hornbills in many green places where it is warm all year round. They live in the thick jungles of Southeast Asia and the open fields of Africa. They like living in various places. Some have flat lands with many trees. Others have hilly areas. Hornbills help plants grow and show that nature is doing well.

Habitats in the Tropics

Hornbills have many homes in the warm parts of the world, and each home is special. They live up high in the rainforest or down low in the open fields. Many kinds of hornbills each like a certain place. This could be a forest full of fruit trees or a place with just a few trees. They are important in the warm parts of the Earth.

Critical Nesting Choices

Hornbills think hard about where to build their homes. It is a big decision. Some hornbills make their homes in tree holes, while others use thick plants or cliff sides. They pick their homes based on how much food is nearby. They also consider if it is safe and if there are good things to build with. They must think about what they need and the hard parts of living in the wild.

Nesting and Sealed Nest Life

When it is time to make a home, hornbills
do something special—they close the nest.
The mommy hornbill stays inside the nest.
She uses mud, spit, and plants to seal it shut
with help from the daddy. The daddy brings
the materials, and the mommy puts it all
together. This keeps the baby birds safe and
makes sure the nest is a good place for them.

Feeding Challenges

While the mommy is in the nest, the daddy must find all the food. He
must travel far to get fruits, bugs, and little animals for his family.
Even if the weather is bad or other animals want the same food, the
hornbill dads work hard. He does this to make sure his family has
enough to eat.

Parental Responsibilities

Hornbills are highly skilled at finding food. The daddies also take
thorough care of their families.

Resourceful Foragers

Daddy hornbills eat many different things to feed their babies. They
eat fruits, bugs, and little animals. This helps them stay alive. It
keeps the forest healthy by spreading seeds and eating bugs.

Journeys for Survival

Every day, the daddy hornbill looks for food in the forest for his family. It is a hard job. He must find his way, stay safe, and get food before other animals do. But he never gives up because he wants to make sure his family is okay.

Nurturing in Isolation

While the daddy is out, the mommy stays in the nest with the eggs and baby birds. She keeps them warm and safe. The daddy and mommy work together to look after their babies in the forest.

Predator Prevention and Nest Defense

The daddy hornbill is like a hero in the jungle. He keeps his family safe from any danger.

Defensive Tactics

Daddy hornbills are very clever. They use different ways to protect their nests. They can make loud noises or act like they are fighting to scare away snakes, monkeys, or big birds. They also pick safe places to build their nests to keep their babies away from dangers.

Guardian Role

The daddy hornbill is always watching for trouble. He is ready at any time to protect his family. It takes courage and hard work. But daddy hornbills do all they can to keep their babies safe. They do it so the babies can grow up strong.

Family Life Beyond the Nest

When the baby hornbills grow up and the nest gets too small, they start to explore the big jungle with their family.

A Family Affair

Once the nest is open, and the chicks are ready to go out, the daddy hornbill still looks after them. He teaches them how to find food and stay safe. The parents show their little ones everything they need to know. Even when the chicks start to do things by themselves, they remember what their daddy taught them.

Flight Training

Learning to fly is a big step for young hornbills. Their daddy is there to help them. He cheers them on as they flap their wings and try to fly. It is hard, but with practice and support, they will soon fly all around the forest, just like their daddy.

Conservation Challenges and Efforts

Hornbills are strong birds. But they have big problems. People are hurting their homes. We need to help protect them.

Threatened Beauty

Hornbills live in pretty places. But those places are in danger from things like cutting down trees. This is making it hard for hornbills to live, and there are fewer of them now. We need to protect their homes.

Global and Local Actions

The good news is that many people around the world want to save the hornbills. They are working together to keep the birds safe and fix their homes. They are saving forests. They are growing new trees. They include people who live near hornbills. When we all

help, we can make sure hornbills have a safe
home for a long time.

Inspiring Young Naturalists

We need to teach kids about nature so they can help protect hornbills for a long time.

Empathy Through Education

When kids learn about hornbills and the forest, they see why it is
important to protect them. They can learn from books, movies, and
games about how everything in nature is connected. When kids care
about hornbills, they will want to help them.

Active Participation

There are many ways kids can help hornbills, like growing trees
or learning about animals. When they share what they know with
others, even more people can help. Every little bit helps, and kids
can change a lot for hornbills and other wildlife.

Discover More About Hornbills

Learning more about hornbills can be fun and helps protect them.

Beyond the Book

There is a lot more to discover about hornbills than what is in books.
You can watch shows about their daily lives, where they live, and

the challenges they face. Online, there are many websites and blogs with the latest hornbill news. There are even apps that make learning about hornbills enjoyable. By exploring these resources, you can understand more about hornbills and their importance.

Advocacy and Support

It is great to learn about hornbills, but helping them is even better. You can join groups that study hornbills and protect their homes. Zoos and bird centers do a lot for hornbills. They care for injured ones and ensure there are enough hornbills. You can help by donating money, becoming a member, or volunteering. Spreading the word about protecting forests and animals can help hornbills too. When you act, you join the team that makes sure hornbills have a bright future.

Conclusion: A Tribute to Hornbill Dads

At the end of our story, we see how amazing hornbill dads are. They work so hard for their families. These birds teach us about love and taking care of the ones we love. They show us how to have strong family bonds and to keep going no matter what.

Hornbill dads are heroes for their families and the whole forest. They remind us to stay together, be strong, and look after nature. Let us remember their lessons about caring for each other and all living things. Let us keep helping hornbill dads and their families, so they can keep flying high for many more years.

Glossary

- **Hornbills:** Big, colorful birds with large beaks that live in the jungle.

- **Habitats:** Places where hornbills or other animals live, like rainforests or open fields.

- **Nesting:** Building a home or nest for eggs and baby birds.

- **Feeding:** Finding and providing food for the family.

- **Parental Responsibilities:** Taking care of and looking after the family.

- **Foragers:** Animals that search for food.

- **Predator:** An animal that hunts and eats other animals.

- **Defensive Tactics:** Ways to protect oneself or one's nest from danger.

- **Guardian:** Someone or something that protects and looks after others.

- **Family Life:** How hornbill families interact and live together.

- **Flight Training:** Learning to fly, with the help of parents.

- **Conservation:** Protecting and preserving nature and wildlife.

Chapter 20: Silky Anteaters – Nurturing in the Canopy

Introduction to Silky Anteaters

Marvels of Nature

Silky anteaters are small, adorable animals that live high in the treetops.

They have shiny, soft fur that looks beautiful when the sunlight hits it. Silky anteaters are good at moving through trees. They fit in well with the green leaves and branches. They get their name from the fact that they eat bugs like ants.

Surprising Protectors

On the treetops, silky anteater dads are excellent at taking care of their babies. These
dads show us that, even in the animal world,
parents can be very caring. They work hard
to keep their little ones safe among the trees
and leaves.

Canopy Habitats: Life in the Treetops

The treetops of tropical forests are like a big,
green playground. There are lots of branches and leaves that make a roof over the
forest. This place is full of life. It has colorful birds and expert climbers, like silky
anteaters.

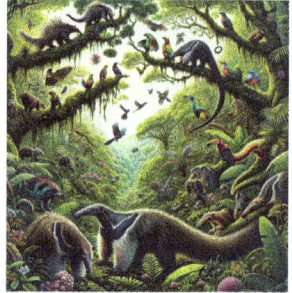

Life in the Treetops

Aerial Haven

The treetops are a safe place for silky anteaters to live. The leaves
give them shelter and lots of places to hide. There are also many
insects, fruits, and sweet plant juices for them to eat. This helps
them stay happy and healthy in their home up high.

Experts in the Treetops

Silky anteaters are perfect for living in trees. They have a strong tail that helps them hold on to branches and claws that help them climb without falling. This lets them move easily and quickly through the trees.

Silky Anteater Parenting

Beginning of Life

When baby silky anteaters are born, they are ready to go! They hold on tight to their dads right away. This keeps them warm and safe.

Paternal Protection

Silky anteater dads are amazing protectors. They keep a close eye on their babies to make sure they are safe on their backs. The dad's back is like a cozy bed for the little ones.

Carrying the Future

Mobile Nursery

Baby silky anteaters ride on their dads' backs. This is like having a moving nursery. It is a safe way for them to see the world and learn about their home on the treetops.

Emotional Connections

The dad and baby anteaters get close when they spend time together. This helps the babies feel secure and learn about life in the trees.

Feeding and Growth

Anteater Diet

Silky anteaters eat ants and must find them in the trees. Dads show their babies how to find ants and teach them to hunt. This helps the babies learn to eat by themselves when they grow up.

Path to Independence

As babies grow, they do more things on their own. Their dads help them learn and encourage them to be brave. This helps them get ready to live on their own on the treetops.

Challenges in the Canopy

Survival Threats

There are many dangers for silky anteaters in the treetops, like birds and snakes that want to eat them. But dads are always watching out for their babies and keeping them safe.

Environmental Pressures

Cutting down the forests is a big problem for silky anteaters. They need the trees to live, and when the forests get smaller, it is harder for them to survive. We need to take care of the forests to help the anteaters.

Adapting to Change

Resilient Species

Silky anteaters are strong and can manage changes in their home. They can live in various places if they need to, which shows they can keep going even when things get tough.

The Human Equation

What we do affects silky anteaters a lot. Building things and cutting down trees can hurt their homes. We need to think about how we can live together with animals like silky anteaters. By taking care of the land and the forests, we can make sure these special animals stay around for a long time.

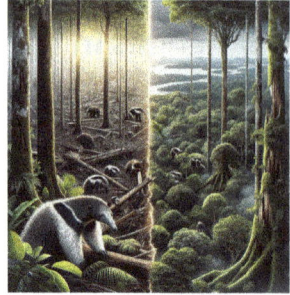

Inspiring Young Nature Enthusiasts

A Call to Wonder

Let us go on an adventure into the amazing world of silky anteaters. Explore the pretty parts of the forest. Learn about the many plants and animals that live there. There are so many interesting things in nature, and every little part of it has its own story. When kids get curious, they start to learn about the world around them. They find out how cool and vital every living thing is.

Active Involvement

You can be a hero to animals and trees! It does not matter how old you are; you can still do important things to help. Learn why forests and wild places are important and tell others about why we need to protect them. If you share and support ideas that help save our environment, you are helping our Earth. This means we will have a beautiful and healthy world now and in the future.

Discover More About Silky Anteaters

Expanding Knowledge

There is so much to learn about silky anteaters. You can study how they live, what they eat, and why they are important to the forest. There are lots of ways to learn more about these special animals and how we can keep them safe.

Guardians of the Forest

You can help protect the forest just like the conservationists do. Try volunteering for groups that save the forest. Join projects that fix damaged parts. Or instruct your friends and family why this is important. Your actions can really help the silky anteaters and the place they call home.

Conclusion: A Tribute to Silky Anteater Dads

In the quiet, green world above the ground, silky anteater dads are like heroes. They take great care of their babies. They do not just follow their instincts. They also teach their little ones and help keep the forest healthy.

These dads are a big part of why the forest is such a wonderful place. So, let us say thank you to them and remember how everyone, even the smallest creatures, is important. We all share the earth, and it is up to us to look after it and all the life it holds. Let us keep the love and care of the silky anteater dads in mind and do our part to take care of our amazing planet.

Glossary

- **Canopy:** Imagine the top part of the forest where the trees stretch up high and make a leafy roof. This roof is full of leaves and branches and is the attic of the forest. It is a fun place where animals like the silky anteater live.

- **Nurturing:** This means helping someone grow by taking safe care of them. Silky anteater fathers are great at nurturing. They take really loving care of their little ones.

- **Habitat:** This is where an animal or plant feels at home. Silky anteaters live in the high treetops of tropical forests.

- **Adaptation:** When plants or animals change to live better in their homes. Silky anteaters have strong tails and sharp claws so they can spend time together in the treetops.

- **Paternal:** This word is all about being a dad. Silky anteater dads show paternal care by keeping their babies safe and feeding them.

- **Mobile Nursery:** This is a way to take care of babies while you are moving around. Baby silky anteaters ride on their dad's back—like having a nursery that goes wherever dad goes!

- **Foraging:** This is when you search for food. Silky anteaters look around the trees to find ants to munch on.

- **Resilient:** Being able to stay strong and get better after something tough happens. Silky anteaters are tough. They can manage changes in their tree-home without giving up.

- **Endangered:** This means there is a danger that we could lose an animal or plant forever. If we hurt the forests, it can make silky anteaters endangered, and we do not want them to disappear.

- **Biodiversity:** This is the mix of various kinds of life you can find in the world or a special place. The canopy is not just for silky anteaters. It is full of many plants and animals. That is what biodiversity is about.

Chapter 21: Ice Guardians: The Harp Seal Fathers

Welcome to the World of Harp Seals

In the cold Arctic, where ice shines and the water is very cold, harp seals live.

They have smooth skin and a thick layer of fat to keep warm. Their fur is silver, gray, and white, which helps them hide in the snow from animals that might want to eat them.

Adapting to the Freezing Cold

Harp seals have big eyes and fur that looks like a harp. These help them see in the not-so-bright Arctic light and stay away from danger.

Dads on Duty

When baby harp seals are born on the ice, their dads play a key role. They watch over the babies to make sure they grow strong in the cold Arctic.

The Ice Cradle: A Nursery for Pups

The Arctic is not just a home for the seals; it is where baby seals are born and grow. The ice is important for them to get bigger and ready for life in the big, icy world.

Early Growth is Key

Baby harp seals need to grow fast to live. With their dads' help, they learn how to move around on the ice and get ready for the ocean.

Together Through Challenges

The first days of the babies' lives are important. Dads are not as caring as moms. But they still help a lot. They keep the babies safe and show them around their cold home.

Fathers: Guardians of the Ice

When it is time to have babies, many harp seals come together on the ice. The dads help protect the babies and take care of the group.

The Importance of Social Life

Male harp seals are important in their groups. They look for mothers for their babies. They also keep everyone safe, especially the little ones.

Working Together

Even though dads are quieter than moms, they are still important. They help keep the ice safe for the babies to grow up well.

Life Beyond the Ice

Working together shows how teamwork is important in nature. Dad's job is vital. The babies learn from them about staying strong and working together in the cold.

Diving into the Arctic Waters

When baby harp seals learn to swim, it is a big step for them in the cold Arctic waters. Their first swim starts their journey through the ice.

Mastering the Icy World

The Arctic waters change a lot, so baby harp seals need to be good swimmers. They need to rest on ice and stay with their group to live.

Beware of the Predators

While swimming, baby harp seals meet dangerous Arctic animals. Being able to dive fast is important, and dads teach them how to stay safe.

Dads Teach Quietly

Dads share their knowledge quietly, which adds to what moms teach. This helps the babies become strong swimmers and stay safe in the Arctic.

Growing into Arctic Swimmers

Learning to swim well is important for baby seals. With their dads' help, they learn how to avoid danger and find their way on the ice.

A Changing Arctic World

The Melting Ice Challenge

The earth is getting warmer, which is bad for the harp seals. The ice where they have their babies is melting, which is dangerous for the babies.

How Climate Change Hurts the Seals

When the Arctic ice melts too fast, baby harp seals lose their safe place. This is bad for them, especially when it is time to have babies.

We Must Help the Seals

Harp seals are in trouble because the Earth is getting warmer. We need to help. We will do this by caring for the environment. We will use clean energy. We will teach others about how climate change affects animals.

Science and People Working Together

We need to study harp seals and how the warm weather affects them to find ways to keep them safe. Telling other people is also important so we can all help our planet.

Looking to the Future

The problems harp seals face remind us that we are connected to the Earth. What we do now can help these animals and our world. We need to act quickly and carefully to protect them.

Hope for Harp Seals

Making a Difference

People everywhere are trying to protect harp seals and their icy homes. There are big efforts to save them and leaders in small places are helping too.

Leadership from Local People

People who have always lived in the Arctic know how to live with nature. They are leading the way to keep the sea and ice safe for seals and other sea animals.

Everyone Must Help with Climate

Agreements like the Paris Agreement are important. They help fight the Earth getting warmer. By reducing pollution, we can help keep the Arctic ice from melting and save the seals' homes.

Good News from Conservation

Good things help keep harp seals and other sea animals safe. Examples include fishing responsibly and making safe places in the ocean.

Science and Speaking Up

Learning about where seals go and how they are doing helps us find the best ways to keep them safe. People who tell others about the seals' problems help get more people to care and help.

A Hopeful Future for Harp Seals

Local people and groups are working to protect the environment. Governments and people all over the world are joining them. They are together bringing hope for the harp seals. Even though they face many problems. There are success stories that make us want to keep working. They inspire us to keep the Arctic full of life.

Unraveling the Secrets of Harp Seals

Discovering the Arctic's Wonders

The world under the Arctic ice is full of secrets, and harp seals are great at living there. We learn a lot about how sea animals can live in such a cold place by watching them.

How Harp Seals Show Evolution's Power

Harp seals are amazing because of how they have changed over time. They have thick fat to keep warm, smooth bodies for swimming fast, and they can dive deep. Learning about them helps us understand how sea animals can live in cold places.

Harp Seals and the Ocean's Life

Harp seals are an important part of the ocean food web. They help keep everything balanced. The way they live can show us how healthy the ocean is.

Protecting the Ocean's Health

Studying harp seals helps us see how everything on Earth is connected. Their actions affect other sea animals and the ocean's health. This helps scientists figure out how to keep the ocean full of life.

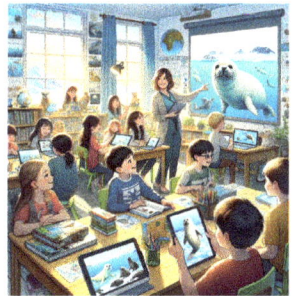

A Starting Point for More Discoveries

Looking at harp seals can lead us to learn more about the deep ocean. They teach us about being tough and adapting, and they make us want to learn more and take care of the environment.

Inspiring New Explorers and Protectors

Learning about harp seals is not just about knowing more. It makes us want to explore and protect our planet. Knowing about these seals makes us love the ocean more and want to keep it safe.

Fun Ideas for Young Learners

A Day in the Life: Harp Seal Pup's Story

Think about what a day would be like for a baby harp seal. Maybe you could write a diary entry as if you were the pup. It could be fun to make up your own stories.

March 10, 2024: My First Day on the Ice

Dear Diary,

Today was amazing. I woke up on the shiny ice, feeling the sun's warmth even though it was cold. My mom looked at me and touched me gently. She taught me a special sound so we can always find each other.

I played with other pups and we ran on the ice. I wasn't very good with my flippers yet, but it was fun. The big ocean called to me, and my mom showed me how to swim. The water was cold, but I felt brave because my mom was with me.

Now the night is here, and I'm cuddling with my mom. The sounds of the ocean tell me there will be more adventures. I can't wait for tomorrow to see more of this icy world.

Goodnight, Diary. I'm excited for the stories tomorrow will bring.

Try It Yourself: Now it is your turn! Imagine you are a harp seal pup. What would you do in the Arctic? Write your own story or draw a picture of your adventure. Share it with friends and see what they think!

This activity makes us creative and helps us feel what it's like to be a harp seal pup. It shows us why it is important to take care of our world.

Arctic Wisdom from Harp Seal Dads

Quiet Teachers in the Arctic

Harp seal dads don't make much noise, but they are important in the Arctic. They watch over their babies and teach them how to live in the cold without saying a word.

Teaching Without Words: Harp Seal Dads Show the Way

Dad seals might not hug or feed the pups like moms do, but they still teach them a lot. They show the pups how to live in the Arctic by what they do, not by talking.

Caretakers of the Ice: Harp Seal Dads Keep Life Going

Harp seal dads do more than just look after their own babies. They help keep the whole Arctic world going. They show us how everything is connected and remind us to take care of each other and the environment.

A Tribute to Toughness and Love

Harp seal dads are strong and kind, even in the very cold Arctic. They show us that being quiet and caring is powerful, and they teach us about love in cold places.

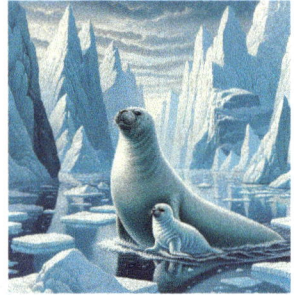

Glossary

- **Arctic:** A very cold place near the North Pole with lots of ice and snow.

- **Harp Seal:** A kind of seal that lives in the Arctic. It has a pattern on its back that looks like a harp and a shiny coat.

- **Ice Sheets:** Big, flat pieces of ice on the sea where harp seals have their families.

- **Pups:** Baby harp seals, which are very cute.

- **Predators:** Animals like polar bears and killer whales that hunt other animals. Harp seals have to be smart to stay away from them.

- **Territory:** The area where an animal lives and that it might protect.

- **Climate Change:** When the weather on Earth changes and

causes problems like less ice for the seals.

- The **Paris Agreement** is a promise. Countries around the world made it to work together to keep the Earth from getting too hot.

Beneath the Vast Sky: Our Ongoing Quest

Our adventure as brave and kind protectors of nature is ending. I, the Sky, say thank you to you, our bold young friends. You will protect our world tomorrow.

We have flown over trees, swum in the sea, walked on ice, and roamed through wild places. We found amazing stories about animal fathers who show us what it means to take care of others.

We watched an alligator look after his babies and a penguin keep warm in the cold. Each story is a piece of the big picture of life on Earth. These stories are not just about staying alive. They show us how love, giving up things for others, and not giving up are found in nature.

As we say goodbye, remember that the sky, the ground, and every place in between have stories to tell. The adventure keeps going and asks you to see more, hear more, and care more.

Take what you have learned from these wonderful animal dads with you. Let their lives make you want to find out more, protect our planet, and be kind. Our Earth's future and all its beautiful things depend on protectors like you.

With hope in our hearts and our eyes on new horizons, let us move toward tomorrow. May the wind whisper to you, the stars show you the way, and the stories of nature give you bravery to keep our Earth safe.

Goodbye, young explorers, and future guardians. The journey does not stop, and the sky is waiting for you to come back to our Earth's never-ending story.

Until we meet again. Keep nature's magic in your hearts. And let the joy of discovery shine in your spirits.

Welcome to being a protector of the wild. Welcome to the next part of your journey.

www.ingramcontent.com/pod-product-compliance
Lightning Source LLC
Chambersburg PA
CBHW062131020426

42335CB00013B/1171